VIVIANE DUNN
& DIANN GRUBER

LISTENING
INTERMEDIATE

OXFORD SUPPLEMENTARY SKILLS

SERIES EDITOR: ALAN MALEY

OXFORD UNIVERSITY PRESS

Oxford University Press
Walton Street, Oxford OX2 6DP

Oxford New York
Athens Auckland Bangkok Bombay
Calcutta Cape Town Dar es Salaam Delhi
Florence Hong Kong Istanbul Karachi
Kuala Lumpur Madras Madrid Melbourne
Mexico City Nairobi Paris Singapore
Taipei Tokyo Toronto

and associated companies in
Berlin Ibadan

Oxford and *Oxford English* are trade marks of
Oxford University Press

ISBN 0 19 453418 9 ✓

© Oxford University Press 1987

First published 1987
Eighth impression 1996

Set by Promenade Graphics Ltd, Cheltenham

Printed in Hong Kong

Illustrations by:

Maggie Silver

The publishers would like to thank the following
for their permission to reproduce photographs:

Associated Press
Bruno Jarret
Jorvik Viking Centre
Musée Rodin, Paris

Studio and location photography by Chris
Honeywell and Rob Judges

The publishers would like to thank the following
for their time and assistance:

Air France
Alitalia
Blackwell's Music Shop, Oxford
British Airways
British Telecommunications PLC South
K.L.M. Royal Dutch Airlines
Midlands and Chilterns District
Oxford and Cambridge Fine Wine Company Ltd
Radio Tees, the independent radio station for the
North East of England
Trans World Airlines
York Archaeological Trust

The words of *Leaving on a jet plane* by John
Denver are reprinted by permission of Cherry
Lane Music Publishing Co. Inc. (c 1967. All rights
reserved).

CONTENTS

Foreword   *vi*

Introduction to the teacher   *vii*

Map of the book   *1*

1   HOW GOOD IS YOUR GEOGRAPHY?   *2*
   1   There's a place . . .   *2*
   2   Your turn   *2*
   3   Right or wrong?   *3*

2   GOING ON A TRIP   *4*
   1   Before the trip   *4*
   2   On the spot   *8*
   3   Next stop   *8*

3   IS ANYBODY THERE?   *10*
   1   Hello?   *10*
   2   I'd like to leave a message . . .   *10*
   3   I saw your ad . . .   *13*

4   TUNING IN   *14*
   1   A mixed bag   *14*
   2   Commercial break   *15*
   3   Door to door   *17*

5   HERE IS THE NEWS   *18*
   1   Do you remember when . . . ?   *18*
   2   People and places   *20*
   3   Take note   *21*

6   RODIN INSIDE OUT   *22*
   1   Outside   *22*
   2   Inside   *24*
   3   What do you think?   *25*

7   A DAY OUT   *26*
   1   What shall we do?   *26*
   2   A voyage of discovery   *28*
   3   Finding out more   *33*

8   LOST: DOG . . .   *34*
   1   The original facts   *34*
   2   Some new information   *38*
   3   The whole story   *40*

Teacher's guide   *41*

Text of the recorded material   *48*

ACKNOWLEDGEMENTS

We would like to thank the following people for their help in the preparation of this book: Janice Abbott, Terri Baker, Emmanuel Desplanques, Francis Dunn, Sydney Dunn, Catherine Gallagher, Sue Girolami, Louis Gruber, Michel Ligier, Michael Swan, Roland Thies, Catherine Walter, Shelley Whittingham, and all our students and colleagues.

FOREWORD

This series covers the four skill areas of Listening, Speaking, Reading and Writing at four levels — elementary, intermediate, upper-intermediate and advanced. Although we have decided to retain the traditional division of language use into the 'four skills', the skills are not treated in total isolation. In any given book the skill being dealt with serves as the *focus* of attention and is always interwoven with and supported by other skills. This enables teachers to concentrate on skills development without losing touch with the more complex reality of language use.

Our authors have had in common the following principles, that material should be:

- creative — both through author-creativity leading to interesting materials, and through their capacity to provoke creative responses from students;
- interesting — both for their cognitive and affective content, and for the activities required of the learners;
- fluency-focused — bringing in accuracy work only in so far as it is necessary to the completion of an activity;
- task-based — rather than engaging in closed exercise activities, to use tasks with pay-offs for the learners;
- problem-solving focused — so as to engage students in cognitive effort and thus provoke meaningful interaction;
- humanistic — in the sense that the materials speak to and interrelate with the learners as real people and engage them in interaction grounded in their own experience;
- learning-centred — by ensuring that the materials promote learning and help students to develop their own strategies for learning. This is in opposition to the view that a pre-determined content is taught and identically internalized by all students. In our materials we do not expect input to equal intake.

By ensuring continuing consultation between and among authors at different levels, and by piloting the materials, the levels have been established on a pragmatic basis. The fact that the authors, between them, share a wide and varied body of experience has made this possible without losing sight of the need to pitch materials and tasks at an attainable level while still allowing for the spice of challenge.

There are three main ways in which these materials can be used:

- as a supplement to a core course book;
- as self-learning material. Most of the books can be used on an individual basis with a minimum of teacher guidance, though the interactive element is thereby lost.
- as modular course material. A teacher might, for instance, combine intermediate *Listening* and *Speaking* books with upper-intermediate *Reading* and elementary *Writing* with a class which had a good passive knowledge of English but which needed a basic grounding in writing skills. *(Alan Maley, Madras 1986)*

INTRODUCTION TO THE TEACHER

Who is this book for?

This book is intended for adult students of English at intermediate level.

What are its aims?

The book is designed to do the following:

- To show students that they can learn to feel at ease with authentic spoken English of the sort they might encounter on the radio or television, over the telephone, or in an overheard conversation.

- To help students develop the strategies and skills necessary for dealing with these types of spoken English.

Which skills does it aim to develop?

Skills such as listening for gist, for recognition, for identification, or for more specific detail are introduced and revised throughout the book. The map on page 1 indicates the skills covered in each unit.

What kinds of recorded material are used?

Semi-authentic, authentic and studio recordings are used. Semi-authentic passages are unscripted dialogue; authentic passages consist of a variety of radio extracts. Several geographical varieties of English have been included.

What kinds of activities are involved?

A wide variety of tasks, activities and exercises are provided in the book, including problem solving, information transfer, gap filling and comprehension questions. In many activities, students are encouraged to use their own knowledge and experience and to express their opinions and preferences. Although all units include either reading or speaking activities, these relate directly to the listening topics and are designed to facilitate the development of listening skills.

How is the book organized?

It consists of eight units of varying length, each with a central topic or theme. Each unit includes several listening passages, introduces or revises several listening skills, and provides activities which promote practice of these skills.

Although the units are intended to be worked through completely and in the order presented, it is possible to isolate individual activities from certain units. Similarly, certain activities could be returned to and exploited differently for revision purposes.

What general principles are followed?

This book is based on the belief that the earlier students are exposed to natural spoken English, the earlier they will abandon their fears of not being able to understand it. In order to allay these initial fears, the tasks in the book have been carefully designed to give students every opportunity to 'get the right answer'. They are encouraged to work in pairs and groups since collaboration can help build self-confidence. Therefore, as they proceed through the units, their confidence in their ability to cope with seemingly difficult passages will grow.

MAP OF THE BOOK

Unit	Title	Topic/theme	Listening skills practised	Listening texts	Pages
1	How good is your geography?	A game about countries	Listening for gist Listening for specific information	Informal conversation	*2–3*
2	Going on a trip	Travel preparations and a European trip	Listening for gist Listening and note-taking Listening and comparing Listening for confirmation Listening and responding	Telephone conversations: —requests for information —making hotel reservations Messages on an answerphone Song	*4–9*
3	Is anybody there?	Messages on an answerphone	Listening for gist Listening for specific information Listening and note-taking Listening and comparing	Messages on an answerphone: —personal —business —in reply to advertisements	*10–13*
4	Tuning in	A few minutes of local radio	Global listening Listening for gist Listening for specific information Listening and reading Listening for confirmation	Local radio extracts: —news —time —weather —advertisements —public information	*14–17*
5	Here is the news	Events in the news	Listening and identifying Listening and note-taking	Famous quotations Radio news items	*18–21*
6	Rodin inside out	A visit to the Rodin Museum in Paris	Listening for gist Listening and identifying Listening for specific information	Informal conversation	*22–25*
7	A day out	A new type of museum	Listening for gist Listening for specific information	Local radio extracts: —advertisements —reports and commentaries Informal commentary	*26–33*
8	Lost: Dog	A local radio station helps to track a lost dog	Listening for specific information Listening for confirmation	A phone-in programme from local radio	*34–40*

1

How good is your geography?

1 There's a place ...

Task 1

📺 Listen to these people. They are all talking about the same subject. What do you think it is? Discuss your ideas with a partner.

2 Your turn

Task 1

How good is your geography?

Here are ten countries. Can you identify them? Choose from the list on the opposite page. Write your answers on line **a** under each picture.

Compare your answers with a partner's.

1 a . . . .
   b . . . .
   c . . . .

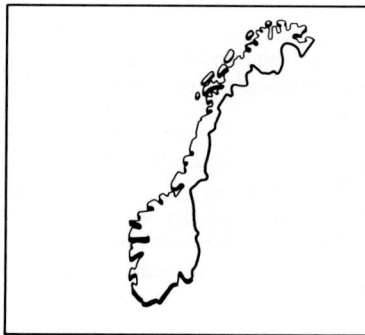

2 a . . . .
   b . . . .
   c . . . .

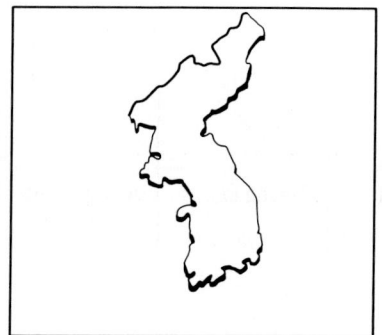

3 a . . . .
   b . . . .
   c . . . .

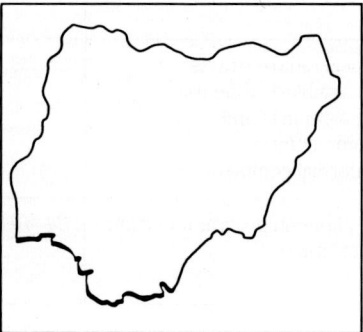

4 a . . . .
   b . . . .
   c . . . .

5 a . . . .
   b . . . .
   c . . . .

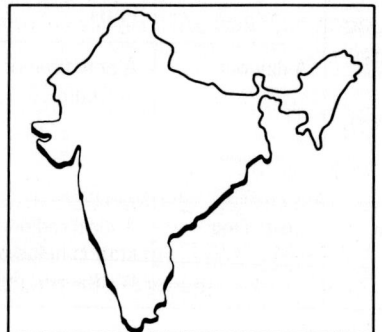

6 a . . . .
   b . . . .
   c . . . .

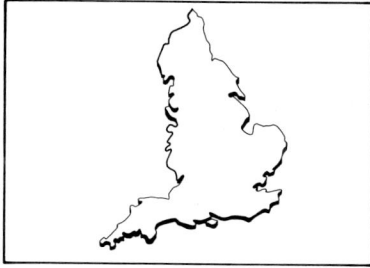

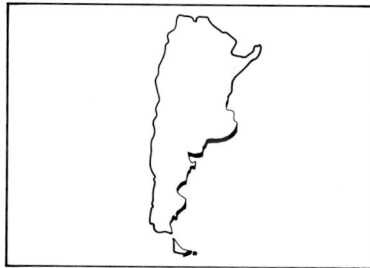

Argentina
Denmark
England
France
India
Iran
Iraq
Japan
Korea
New Zealand
Nigeria
Norway
Portugal
Spain
Sweden

7   a   . . . .

    b   . . . .

    c   . . . .

8   a   . . . .

    b   . . . .

    c   . . . .

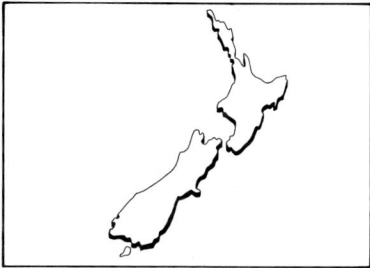

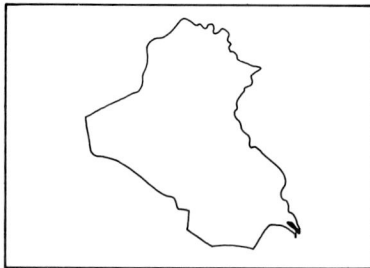

9   a   . . . .

    b   . . . .

    c   . . . .

10   a   . . . .

    b   . . . .

    c   . . . .

3   Right or wrong?

Task 1

Listen to Steve and Liz. Steve is playing the 'How good is your geography?' game. Write Steve's answers on line **b** under your answers.

Task 2

Now listen to Liz telling Steve the correct answers. Write them on line **c**. Be careful, she gives the answers in a different order.

> How many correct answers did you have? How many did Steve have? So how good *is* your geography?
>
> **Score:**
> 9–10   Excellent. You really know your geography.
>   6–8   Nobody's perfect!
>   3–5   Buy an atlas!
>   0–2   Don't play this sort of game again!

2

Going on a trip

1 Before the trip

Task 1

What are some of the things that you do before going on a trip to another country or to another part of your own country?

Discuss your ideas with a partner.

Task 2

📠 Listen to two telephone conversations. What aspect of preparing for a trip is involved?

Task 3

📠 Listen to three telephone conversations. Imagine that you are the person making the telephone calls. Take notes on the information you receive.

Task 4

Look at the five timetables. Some of them contain information that was requested in the telephone conversations in Task 3.

Use your notes from Task 3 to match each conversation with a timetable. Compare your answers with a partner's and listen to the conversations again if necessary.

Frankfurt (GMT +2)

Reservations 25650
Air Freight 691-054
🏨 Frankfurt Inter-Continental
FH Forum Wiesbaden

To LONDON 🏨FH Heathrow

Daily	1230	1405	**121** Nonstop
			Above Flt Eff 30 Sep
Daily	1400	1435	**121** Nonstop
			Above Flt Dis After 29 Sep
Daily	1745	1815	**143** Nonstop
			Above Flt Departs 1645 Eff 30 Sep

a

DEPARTS DE LUXEMBOURG/Departures from/Abflüge ab Luxembourg

vers to nach	Validité Validity Gültigkeit	Jours Days Tage	Dép. Dep. Abfl.	Arr. Arr. Ank.	Rep. Meal Mahl	No. vol Flt. Nbr. Flug Nr.
NICE	04.11.84–24.03.85	⑦	12.00	14.30	M	LG 251
	30.03.85	⑥	12.00	14.30	M	LG 251
ORLANDO International	02.11.84–29.03.85	⑤	14.00	19.55	M/M	FI 665 ⑨
PALMA *	29.10.84–05.11.84 ①		12.35	14.35	M	LG 615
	19.11.84+26.11.84 ①		12.35	14.35	M	LG 615
	10.12.84 ①		12.35	14.35	M	LG 615
	24.12.84–25.03.85 ①		12.35	14.35	M	LG 615
	30.03.85	⑥	07.05	09.05	B	LG 601
	03.11.84–30.03.85	⑥	14.45	16.40	S	LG 613
PARIS CHARLES DE GAULLE (Aérogare 1)		①②③④⑤⑥⑦	07.40	08.40	B	LG 201 ①
		①②③④⑤	10.50	11.50	D	LG 205 ①
	29.10.84–29.03.85 ①②③④⑤		14.40	15.40	D	LG 207 ①
	29.10.84–29.03.85 ①②③④⑤⑥⑦		18.45	19.45	D	LG 203 ②
REYKJAVIK	30.10.84–30.03.85 ② ④⑤⑥		13.30	16.00	M	FI 615
	01.11.84–28.03.85 ④		14.00	16.30	M	FI 621
	—		—	—		—
ROME	31.10.84–27.03.85 ③		13.00	14.50	M	LG 553
	29.10.84–29.03.85 ① ⑤		18.00	19.50	M	LG 551 ⑤
SALZBOURG *	22.12.84–09.03.85	⑥	09.45	10.55	D	LG 381
TENERIFE SUR REINA SOFIA °	01.11.84–28.03.85 ④		09.00	12.30	D/M	LG 711
TUNIS	03.11.84–30.03.85	⑥	14.30	16.50	M	TU 639

b

c

days of operation	dep.	arr.	flight — type class
From AMSTERDAM (cont.) to			
VIENNA ⊗			
Mo Tu We Th Fr – Su	0805	0945	KL 255 CM D9S
– – – – – Sa –	1205	1345	OS 484 FY D9S
Oct 28 — Dec 15			
– – – – – Sa –	1205	1445	OS 488 FY D9S
Dec 22 — Mar 30			
– We – – – –	1255	1440	KL 889 FCM 74M
– – – – – Sa –	1930	2110	KL 567 CM D8S
Oct 28 — Jan 19			
– – – – – Sa –	1930	2110	KL 567 CM 310
Jan 26 — Mar 30			
Mo Tu We Th Fr – Su	2055	2235	OS 486 FY D9S

d

ヨーロッパ(北回り・モスクワ経由) EUROPE(POLAR ROUTE・VIA MOSCOW)

G.M.T.との時間差 Difference from G.M.T.	曜日 DAY 便名 FLIGHT NO. 機種 AIRCRAFT クラス CLASS	Mo 413 B747 PCY	We.Su 415 B747 PCY	Fr 427 B747 PCY	Su 427 B747 PCY	Sa 425 B747 PCY	Mo 425 B747 PCY	Fr 403 B747 PCY	Mo.Tu We ⊠ 423 B747 PCY	Th.Fr Sa 421 B747 PCY	Tu.Th Sa 433 B747 PCY	Th 441 B747 PCY	Su 443 B747 PCY	Fr 447 B747 PCY	Daily 52 DC10 Y
+9	大阪 OSAKA ……発dp	1920	1920	1920	1920			1920	1920	1920	1920	1920			
+9	東京(成田) TOKYO(NARITA) {着ar 発dp	2030 2130	2030 2130	2030 2130	2030 2230	2100	2030 2130	2030 2230	2030 2230	2030 2130		0940 ↑※ (152) DC10	0940 ↑※ (152) DC10	0940 ↑※ (152) DC10	1530
	日付変更線 International Date Line														
−9	アンカレジ ANCHORAGE {着ar 発dp	1000 1130	1000 1130	1000 1130	1100 1230	0930 1100	1000 1130	1000 1130	1100 1230	1000 1130		1045 1200	1045 1200	1045 1200	1635
+3	モスクワ MOSCOW {着ar 発dp	0555 0705										1615 1725	1615 1725	1615 1725	
+1	コペンハーゲン COPENHAGEN {着ar 発dp														
+1	ハンブルク HAMBURG ⊕{着ar 発dp														
+1	アムステルダム AMSTERDAM {着ar 発dp	0620 0730							0620 0730		0605 0720				
+1	フランクフルト FRANKFURT ⊕……着ar														
0	ロンドン LONDON ⊕{着ar 発dp										0825				
+1	パリ PARIS {着ar 発dp					0615 0730 0935	0615					1840			
+1	チューリヒ ZURICH ……着ar	0640 0750	0740 0850	0610	0640	0835					1815				
+1	ローマ ROME ……着ar	0855 0955									1915				
+1	マドリード MADRID ……着ar	0935	0950												

e

From	Air-port	Dep.	Arr.	Flight	Cl.	A/C	Transfer Arr.	At	Dep.	Flight	Cl.	A/C	Note
LONDON LON UNITED KINGDOM													Tel 01-7344020
ÅARHUS AAR													
DX6	LGW	1740✕	2020	SK 506CMB D9S									NONSTOP
STOCKHOLM ARN				**SAS HOTEL**									
D	LHR	1145✕	1505	SK 526CMB D9S									NONSTOP
FROM 28OCT D	LHR	1835	2155	SK 528CMB D9S									NONSTOP
UNTIL 27OCT D	LHR	1935	2155	SK 528CMB D9S									NONSTOP
FROM 28OCT D	LHR	0855	1220	BA 650 CML 73S									NONSTOP
FROM 28OCT D	LHR	1425	1750	BA 652 CML 73S									NONSTOP
UNTIL 27OCT DX6	LGW	1620	1850	BA 652 CML 73S									NONSTOP
UNTIL 26OCT DX6	LGW	1635	2005	BA 654 CML 73S									
FROM 28OCT D	LGW	1705	2030	BA 654 CML 73S									

LOS ANGELES LAX
CALIFORNIA, U.S.A.   Tel 213-655-8600

Task 5

One of the things you probably mentioned in your discussion about preparations for a trip is reserving a hotel room. Read the letters below and then listen to a telephone conversation in which someone is reserving a room. Which of the three letters was sent after the conversation to confirm the reservation?

Hotel Belmont
Como
Italia

60 Amagor Boulevard
DK 2300 Copenhagen S.
October 30, 1984

Dear Sir or Madam,

This is in confirmation of the reservation of a single room with shower and private toilet for Sunday, 4th November in the name of Mr. Bassanno.

Yours truly,

G. Lakes

a

Hotel Belmont
30 Rue du Bassanno
Paris 75016
FRANCE

S.F.C.
45, bd.   Prince Henry
L-1724 Luxembourg
October 31, 1984

Dear Sirs,

Following our telephone conversation of 30th October, I would like to confirm the reservation of a single room with bath for Mr. Lakes who will be arriving in Paris on Sunday evening, 4th November.

Yours faithfully,

R Jones

GL/rj

b

Hotel Bassano
30, Rue Belmont
Paris 16
France

38, Queen's Road
London N11
29.10.84

Dear Sir,
          I am writing to confirm the reservation of a double room at 458F for Mr & Mrs. Lakes on Saturday 3rd November.

          Yours sincerely,

          Lake

c

Task 6

Look back at the timetables in Task 4.

What is the connection between one of the timetables and the letter you chose in Task 5? Discuss your ideas with a partner.

Use all the information you have collected to fill in this luggage label for the person who is going on a trip.

⊕ LUXAIR

NAME: ⎯⎯⎯⎯⎯⎯⎯⎯⎯⎯⎯⎯⎯⎯⎯⎯⎯⎯⎯⎯⎯⎯

ADDRESS: ⎯⎯⎯⎯⎯⎯⎯⎯⎯⎯⎯⎯⎯⎯⎯⎯⎯⎯⎯

DESTINATION: ⎯⎯⎯⎯⎯⎯⎯⎯⎯⎯⎯⎯⎯⎯⎯⎯

FLIGHT NUMBER: ⎯⎯⎯⎯⎯⎯⎯⎯⎯⎯⎯⎯⎯

Task 7

Before starting on his trip, Mr Lakes telephoned a friend in Paris twice. Each time his friend was out and he left a message on the answerphone. What do you think he said?

Discuss your ideas with a partner and then listen to the two messages and compare them with your ideas.

2   On the spot

Task 1

While he was in Paris, Mr Lakes stayed in two different hotels. Why do you think he changed hotels? Discuss your ideas with a partner.

📼 Now listen to two messages on his friend's answerphone (his friend was still out!) to find out what his reason for moving was.

Task 2

📼 Listen to the following four telephone conversations. What happens in each one? Which one offers a solution to Mr Lakes' hotel problem?

Task 3

In fact, during his stay in France, Mr Lakes stayed in four different hotels. Each time he moved he rang his friend to say where he was, but she was out.

📼 Listen to the messages on the answerphone and match the information on the right to the hotels.

Hotel Belmont   Room 22
Hotel Templer   till Thursday
Hotel Beaux Arts   Lyon
Hilton Hotel   Orly Airport
                         720 65 05
                         Room 406
                         till Sunday
                         till Tuesday
                         687 33 88

3   Next stop

Task 1

Mr Lakes is going to London next.

Look at the timetable on the opposite page and identify:

1   the name of the airport of departure . . . .
2   the name of the airport of arrival . . . .
3   the number of flights it is possible to take on a Tuesday . . . .
4   the telephone number for information and reservations . . . .

British Caledonian

FROM PARIS (Charles de Gaulle) FRANCE
Check−in : −20 mins.
☎ 261 50 21

Frequency	Dep.	Flt. No.	A/c	Class	Stops	Arr.
To **LONDON** (Gatwick) U.K.		**B.CAL.JET**				
Mo to Fr	0800	**BR881**	B11	Y	Non-stop	0800
		Above Flight Does Not Operate On Dec25,Dec26,Dec27,Dec28,Dec31,Jan 1				
Daily	1000	**BR883**	B11	Y	Non-stop	1000
		Above Flight Does Not Operate On Dec24,Dec25,Dec26,Dec27,Dec28,Dec29,Dec30,Dec31,Jan 1				
Daily	1200	**BR885**	B11	Y	Non-stop	1155
		Above Flight Does Not Operate On Dec25,Dec26				
FrSu	1500	**BR887**	B11	Y	Non-stop	1455
Daily	1730	**BR893**	B11	Y	Non-stop	1725
		Above Flight Does Not Operate On Dec25				
Daily	1955	**BR895**	B11	Y	Non-stop	1955
		Above Flight Does Not Operate On Dec25				

Task 2

📼 Mr Lakes' assistant is telephoning British Caledonian in Paris. Listen to her telephone enquiry and imagine that you are the airline employee. Can you answer her questions? Listen once completely first.

Task 3

📼 Now listen to both sides of the conversation and compare the employee's answers with your own.

Task 4

📼 Listen to the song. What is it about? Do you think it is happy or sad? Why?

Discuss your ideas with the rest of the class. What title would you give the song?

3

Is anybody there?

1 Hello?

Task 1

Listen to the two short extracts. Why were they recorded?

In pairs, discuss these questions:

- Do you use this sort of recording?
- Do you know anyone else who does?
- How do you feel when you hear one?

2 I'd like to leave a message . . .

Task 1

Catherine, Thomas and Julie are friends who share a flat. Each evening when they come home from work, they listen to the messages on their answerphone.

Listen to one day's messages. How many were there for each person?

Catherine . . . .

Thomas . . . .

Julie . . . .

Task 2

Some of the messages which people left were in answer to notices or advertisements which the friends had put up.

Read the advertisements with a partner. What is each one offering or asking for?

a

TO LET

2 ROOM APARTMENT
SMALL, BUT COMFORTABLE
QUIET NEIGHBOURHOOD
REASONABLE RENT
TEL. 4373-52-45
LEAVE A MESSAGE FOR JULIE

c

b

WEEKEND in AMSTERDAM

I'm looking for someone to share car expenses. Leaving on Friday 9th and returning Sunday 11th. Interested? Call Thomas on 4373-52-45 and leave a message

Do you speak French with a funny accent?

———— Lose it! ————

I can help you: I'm bilingual in French and English and have lots of teaching experience.

Call Catherine 4373-52-45 & leave a message.

Now listen to the messages in Task 1 again. Which ones are clearly in answer to advertisements?

	i	*ii*	*iii*	*iv*	*v*	*vi*
a						
b						
c						
no ad.						

Task 3

Listen to five messages in which the callers do not say the name of the person they are leaving a message for. Look at the advertisements again and fill in the table to show who each message was for.

Message no.	Catherine	Thomas	Julie
i			
ii			
iii			
iv			
v			

Task 4

Catherine always returns business calls before answering personal ones. Listen to five messages for her. Which ones are personal calls?

Task 5

Listen to Catherine's four business messages again. For each one note down the information that she needs before returning the call. Some of the information is already given in the table below. Add any other information you hear. Don't worry if you can't fill every box.

	Name of caller	*Reason for calling*	*Phone number*	*Best time to call back*
i	Andrea Gibson			
ii	Sally Edgar			
iii				
iv		wants an intensive French course		

3 I saw your ad . . .

Task 1

Look at these advertisements in pairs. What is each one offering?

URGENT!

FOR SALE

Canon AE1
and 50mm lens.

VERY CHEAP!

Tel: 3257 0100

FOR SALE

PEUGEOT 104

1984 20,000 KM in perfect condition.
Complete record of maintenance
Call 4218 85 66

Would you like to spend a week
APPLE-PICKING?
No pay, but free board & lodging
Lots of fresh air and as many
apples as you can carry home!
Call **4621 67 35**
(Hurry apples are
ripe now!)

Task 2

Form small groups and choose one of the advertisements.

Listen to the eight answerphone messages once. In your group, decide how many of the messages are answers to your advertisement.

Listen again and take notes on the information given in *your* messages. Don't worry if you can't write down all of the information. Compare notes in your group and listen again if you disagree.

Task 3

Exchange notes with another group. Play the messages again but this time listen to the ones which correspond to the notes you have been given. Add to or correct any of the information in the notes.

4

Tuning in

1   A mixed bag

Task 1

You are going to hear some extracts from the radio.
🔈 Listen and count the number of extracts you hear. For each new extract, tick (√) a box.

1	2	3	4						

Task 2

🔈 Listen to the extracts again and identify each one in the table below.

	News	Time	Advertisement	Public information	Weather
1					
2					
3					
4					

2 Commercial break

Task 1

Listen to the five advertisements from Section 1 again.
Which pictures represent the same type of product or service as the advertisements?

Number the pictures in the order that you hear the advertisements.

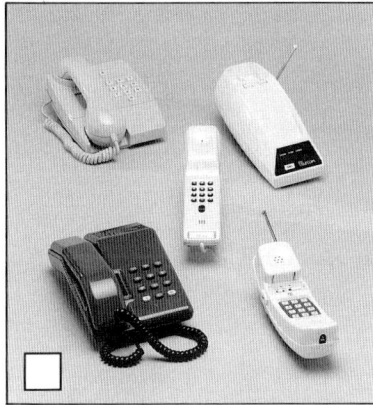

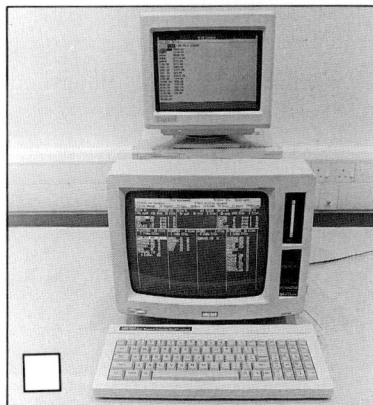

Task 2

Read these questions. Try to answer them as you listen to the advertisements again.

Advertisement 1

a   Complete this sentence:

'At Penta we try . . . . to make buying a used car

. . . . and . . . . for you.'

b   Penta is open ☐ every day.

☐ every day except Sundays.

☐ until 7 p.m.

Advertisement 2

a   Charles Church are offering cheese and wine when you visit their

show-house ☐ every day from 9–5 p.m.

☐ every evening and Saturday all day.

☐ on Friday evening and Saturday all day.

                                                                    T   F

b   The new show-house is opposite a cricket club. ☐ ☐

Advertisement 3

a   The Slimtel costs ☐ £28.85

☐ £39.95

☐ £29.95

b   Complete the opening times of the British Telecom Phone Shop.

Mondays to Fridays . . . . . . to . . . . . .

Saturdays . . . . . . to . . . . . .

Advertisement 4

a   *Finder* magazine is published ☐ once a month.

☐ once a week.

☐ every day.

                                                                    T   F

b   *Finder* is a financial news magazine. ☐ ☐

Advertisement 5

a   Tick the towns you hear:

☐ Pisa	☐ Venice	☐ Verona
☑ Milan	☐ Naples	☐ Turin
☐ Florence	☐ Rome	☐ Bologna

b   How many flights are there to Milan?

☐ 2 per day

☐ 3 per day

☐ 3 per week

3   Door to door

Task 1

This is part of an advertising song.
Listen and follow the words in your book.

'*. . . it is the best to buy.*
Let's not talk, instead I'll show you why.
But how, how can I make this clear
With you in there and me out here?

I'm gonna knock on your door,
Ring on your bell,
Tap on your window too.
Come on and open your door so I can show you more,
I'm gonna knock and ring and tap until you do.'

In pairs, discuss who is talking and who he is talking to.

What do you think this song is advertising?
In pairs, make a list of possibilities.

. . . .

. . . .

. . . .

Task 2

Listen to another part of the same song and make changes to your
list if necessary.

Task 3

Now listen to some more of the same song. What is the song
advertising?

5

Here is the news

1 Do you remember when . . .?

Task 1

Read these famous English and American quotations. In pairs, match each quotation with the name of the person who said it.

a '. . . an iron curtain has descended across the continent . . .'

b '. . . That's one small step for a man; one giant leap for mankind . . .'

c '. . . I am the greatest!'

d '. . . I have a dream . . .'

e '. . . We're more popular than Jesus . . .'

f '. . . ask not what your country can do for you, ask what you can do for your country.'

g '. . . without the help and support of the woman I love.'

Martin Luther King
Muhammad Ali
John Lennon
Neil Armstrong
Edward VIII
Winston Churchill
John F. Kennedy

Task 2

Listen to five extracts from famous speeches which were broadcast on the radio. Each extract includes one of the quotations above. Which quotation is from which speech? Write the number of the extract next to the quotation which comes from it.

Task 3

Try to guess the approximate date and context of each quotation. Discuss your ideas in pairs and listen again if necessary. You can check your answers on page 64.

Task 4

Match each of the photographs below to the headline which represents the same event. Write the letter of the photograph next to the appropriate headline.

a

d

b

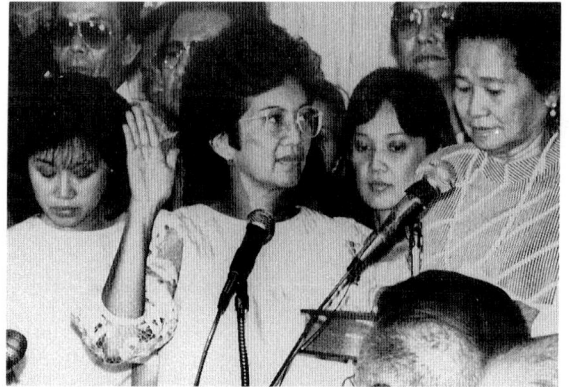

e

c

1 SHCHARANSKY FREED WITH 8 OTHERS IN BERLIN EXCHANGE

2 MARCOS QUITS; US RECOGNIZES AQUINO

3 US SPACE SHUTTLE EXPLODES ON TAKE-OFF

4 Nuclear accident at Soviet plant causes injury

5 Bomb kills four on TWA plane; jet lands safely

Task 5

Now listen to three news reports. Write the extract number next to the appropriate headline on page 20.

Compare your answers with a partner's. Do you agree? Listen again for key words to support your opinion.

2   People and places

Task 1

Listen to three extracts from the radio news. For each one, note down any important words that you hear. Don't worry if you can't fill every box. Some of the information is already provided for you.

People	Places	Other important words
	Windsor	
		EEC NATO
Mrs W. W. Simpson		sad, lonely old woman

Task 2

In pairs, compare the words you wrote in the table. Listen again to check them, if necessary.

Try to guess which event each extract describes.

3   Take note

Task 1

Look at these words with a partner. Use a dictionary, or ask your
teacher about any words you don't know.

ban	cesium 137	Chernobyl	contamination	flocks
Kiev	Lake District	lamb	minister	power station
Russia	safe	sell	three weeks	Wales

Task 2

Listen to another extract from the news. Circle any of the words
above that you hear in the extract. Compare your answers with a
partner's.

Use the words you circled and try to re-tell the news report
together.

Task 3

Listen to three news reports from 1978. For each one:

- listen and individually note down key words that you hear
- share your notes with the other students and make a list of
  everyone's words on the blackboard
- listen again to check the key words
- identify the event and then re-tell it using the words on the
  blackboard.

Task 4

Listen to the international news on the radio (on the BBC or the
Voice of America, for example) and use the instructions in Task 3 to
identify the day's events.

6

Rodin inside out

1 Outside

Task 1

Here are four works by the French sculptor, Rodin. What do you think each one represents? Compare your ideas with a partner's.

a

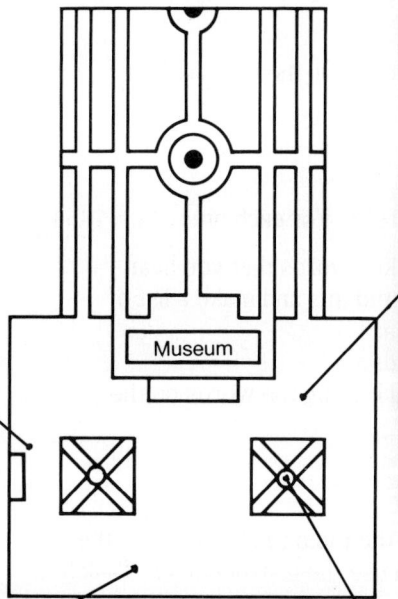

Museum

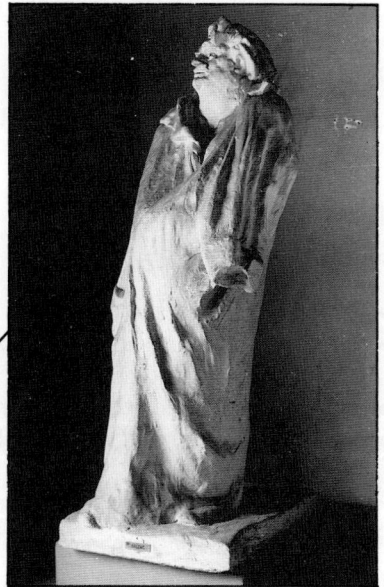

d

b

c

Task 2

Two people, one American and one British, are visiting the park at the Rodin Museum in Paris. They are discussing the works you can see opposite. Listen to their conversation and number the works in order as they are discussed.

Task 3

Here are some comments and questions the visitors had about the four works. Try to guess which work each refers to, then listen again to check your ideas.

Comments	*Questions*
☐ 'Maybe he's a Greek god or something.'	☐ 'Did they (die)?'
☐ 'What is it? A door or a gate or something . . .'	☐ 'So it was a controversial statue, this one?'
☐ 'The city was under siege, I think . . .'	☐ 'What's The Thinker doing up there?'
☐ '. . . and then they didn't want it after he made it . . .'	☐ 'What's he thinking about?'
☐ 'It was something about the Hundred Years' War, wasn't it? That was when it took place . . .'	
☐ 'It must tell a story, mustn't it? . . . goodness knows what the story is!'	
☐ 'An athlete, probably. I mean . . . look at the size of the legs . . .'	

Task 4

When they went into the museum building, the visitors bought a catalogue and talked again about the works they had seen in the park. Listen to their discussions and tick (√) the *comments* in Task 3 which are confirmed.

Compare your ideas with a partner's, then try to answer the *questions* in Task 3 together.

2   Inside

Task 1

Here are three works by Rodin which the two visitors particularly liked. What do you think of them?

1   2   3

Task 2

The names of these works are:

a *The Secret*
b *The Cathedral*
c *The Hand of God.*

Which name do you think goes with each statue?

Task 3

Now listen to the two visitors discussing the three works. Number the pictures in order as the people talk about them, then compare your ideas with a partner's.

Check your ideas in Task 2. Listen again if necessary.

3   What do you think?

Task 1

Here are four more works by Rodin. Look at them alone or with a partner. Are there any that you particularly like or dislike? Can you say why you like or don't like each one?

Young woman with Flowers in her Hat (1865–1870)

Torso (1877–1878)

Head of Pain (1882)

Task 2

The two visitors saw these works during their afternoon at the museum. Listen to their conversation and note down which ones the woman likes and which ones the man likes. Listen carefully because they do not discuss the works in order.

Task 3

Compare your answers with a partner's. How do the visitors' tastes in statues compare with yours?

The Idyll of Ixelles (1876)

7

A day out

1 What shall we do?

Task 1

What sort of things do you do at weekends, on holiday, or when you are visiting another country?

Exchange ideas with a partner. How do different weather conditions affect what you do, e.g. a sunny morning, a rainy afternoon, etc.?

What sort of things do other people do which you have not included in your discussion?

Task 2

Listen to four short radio extracts on places to visit or things to do. What sort of places or activities do they refer to? Tick (√) the correct items in the following list:

☐	zoo	☐	fashion show
☐	dance	☐	motorbike race
☐	exhibition	☐	bowling alley
☐	motor show		

Would you like to go to any of these? Discuss your opinions in pairs.

Task 3

Look at these advertisements for places to go or things to do.

- What sort of place or activity is advertised in each one?
- What town is each place or activity in?

1   2

3

Return to the 10th Century England's Viking Age

TWELFTH CEN
THIRTEENTH CEN
FOURTEENTH CEN
FIFTEENTH CENTURY
SIXTEENTH CENTURY
SEVENTEENTH CENTURY
EIGHTEENTH CENTURY
NINETEENTH CENTURY
TWENTIETH CENTURY

JORVIK VIKING CENTRE

Coppergate YORK YO1 1NT Telephone (0904) 643211 Telex: 7623 Jorvik G
from 14th April 1984 7 days a week from 9 am

4

Live Entertainment at an all inclusive price

Dolphin & Killer Whale Shows

High Dive Spectacular from USA
(15th April – 10th Sept only)

7 Drive Through Animal Reserves

Licensed Bars Restaurants & Picnic Areas

Parrot Show

Children's Farmyard and Amusements

Windsor Safari Park and Seaworld

Open daily from 10.00 am

HEVER CASTLE

near Edenbridge, Kent.

IS WAITING FOR YOU WITH

a spectacular Heritage Show every month (April–October)

first-ever Heritage Flower Festival (June)

International Jousting Tournament (September)

Anne Boleyn's childhood home is open to visitors daily except Thursdays, 1 April–30 September, 12 noon to 5.00.

SPECIAL PARTY VISITS THURSDAYS AND EVENINGS, ALL YEAR.

Enquiries – Edenbridge (0732) 862205.

5

6

THE VIKINGS ARE HERE.

Though their violent raids are legendary, the Vikings were the greatest explorers, traders and settlers of their age. Now for the first time you can discover the many aspects of Viking life at the British Museum. See how they lived, their magnificent craftwork, their traded and looted treasures, jewellery, sword blades. Byzantine silks and Viking ship relics. It is an exhibition unlikely ever to be repeated. See it for yourself and discover the fascinating world of the Vikings.

THE VIKINGS at THE BRITISH MUSEUM
Until 20 July

For opening times see classified columns. Closed 4 April and 5 May
SPONSORED BY THE TIMES AND SUNDAY TIMES in association with SAS Scandinavian Airlines and the Nordic Council.
The BBC film series VIKINGS coincides with the exhibition.

Task 4

🔊 Listen to this extract from local radio news. Which of the places or activities advertised in Task 3 does it refer to?

2   A voyage of discovery

Task 1

The Jorvik Viking Centre was built as a result of archaeological excavations in York which were begun in 1976. The Centre was built on the site of the excavations and was opened in April 1984.

The excavations gave an interesting insight into how the Vikings lived, and the first thing visitors to the Centre see is information about who the Vikings were.

What is *your* image of the Vikings? Which of the pictures below corresponds most to your image of the Vikings? Use the words above the pictures to exchange ideas about them.

WHO WERE THE VIKINGS?

Traders

Settlers

Raiders

Conquerors

Town builders

Seafarers

Craftsmen

Task 2

Look at the pictures again and listen to part of a recorded commentary on Jorvik. Which of the pictures corresponds to the image of the Vikings as given in the recording?

Task 3

Listen once through to a description of Viking trade and the standard of living at the time the Vikings were in York.

Task 4

Listen again and do the following activities as you listen.

Trade

Tick (√) the items which the Vikings imported.

☐ amber
☐ jewellery
☐ wine
☐ beer
☐ tools
☐ skins

Standard of living

Complete the missing words.

'*They were enjoying a very comfortable standard of living,*

nice . . . ., ... *things* . . . ., ...

They would be very comfortably off by our standards.'

Tick the sentence below which has the same meaning as 'They would be very comfortably off by our standards'.

☐ The Vikings were relatively rich compared with present-day standards of living.

☐ The Vikings were relatively poor compared with present-day standards of living.

Task 5

Look at the various extracts about Jorvik below. They are taken from advertisements, tourist magazines and brochures. What impressions do they give you about:

- the sort of place the Jorvik Viking Centre is?
- how new and interesting this type of museum is?

The most exciting journey in a thousand years

Journey Through Time

"*The most exciting tourism project yet seen in this country*".

When you visit the Jorvik Viking Centre at York you go back in time to see, hear and even smell this part of the city of Jorvik as it was 1,000 years ago.

The Jorvik Viking Centre, a revolutionary concept in museum design.

It was happening 1000 years ago — and it's happening now. In Jorvik.
All the sights, sounds and smells are yours to experience. A subterranean 'time-car' will take you backwards in time from Coppergate, York, to leave you 1000 years in the past.

Task 6

Read this paragraph from the Jorvik Viking Centre Official
Guidebook.

**In the Jorvik Viking Centre <u>people from the 20th century journey back in time to the 10th century</u>. The
journey is done in time cars, which silently glide back through the years, past some of the thirty or so
generations of York's people who have walked the pavements of Coppergate, until time stops, on a late
October day in 948. For a while modern time travellers explore Coppergate and a little alley, Lundgate,
which runs off it. The neighbourhood is full of the sights and sounds and smells of 10th century Jorvik.
<u>Townspeople are there, buying and selling, working and playing.</u>**

The three pieces of information which are underlined in the
paragraph are also contained in a continuation of the radio extract
you heard in Task 4.

Listen to the rest of the extract and number the underlined parts of
the guide book in the order that you hear the same information.
Listen carefully, the information is expressed differently on the tape!

What sort of impression do you have of the Jorvik Viking Centre
now? What do you think you can see there? Exchange ideas with a
partner.

Task 7

Viv and Michel are visiting Jorvik and travelling through the Viking
village in one of the electronically-controlled time cars. There is a
recorded commentary in English, but Michel doesn't understand
much English so Viv occasionally comments on the things they see,
or repeats the information from the commentary.

Look at the pictures of the Viking village on page 32 as you listen to
their conversation. Number the scenes in the order in which Viv
mentions them.

Task 8

Now listen to a radio reporter's commentary as he travels through
Jorvik. He comments on some of the same things that Viv
commented on in Task 7.

Look at the pictures of the Viking village on page 32 as you listen and
put a cross next to the scenes which are mentioned by both Viv and
the reporter.

a ☐

b ☐

c ☐

d ☐

e ☐

f ☐

g ☐

h ☐

i ☐

3 Finding out more

If you have developed an interest in Jorvik, this page is for you! The passage below, adapted from the *Jorvik Viking Centre Official Guide* will recapitulate some of the things you already know and tell you some things you don't. The information at the bottom of the page will be useful if you ever have a chance to go to the North of England and want to visit Jorvik.

JORVIK, LOST VIKING CAPITAL

A thousand years ago York was one of the largest, richest and most famous cities in the whole of Britain. People in the 10th century called it JORVIK and knew it as the capital of the North of England, and one of Europe's greatest trading ports. It owed its prosperity to the hard work and commercial enterprise of Viking settlers from Scandinavia who had captured it in AD 866 and almost totally rebuilt it.

Viking Jorvik has now completely disappeared. In some parts of modern York, however, archaeologists have found that remains of Jorvik do still survive. They are buried deep below the streets and buildings of the 20th century city. Whole streets of houses, shops and workshops are to be found.

Between 1976 and 1981 archaeologists from the York Archaeological Trust excavated a part of this lost city. The dig took place in Coppergate. The remains were so well preserved that every aspect of life at the time could be reconstructed. The York Archaeological Trust decided to tell the story of Jorvik as it was a thousand years ago. To do so it built the Jorvik Viking Centre in the huge hole created by the dig.

In the Jorvik Viking Centre people from the 20th century journey back in time to the 10th century. The journey is done in time cars, which silently glide back through the years, past some of the thirty or so generations of York's people who have walked the pavements of Coppergate until time stops, on a late October day in 948. For a while modern travellers explore Coppergate and a little alley, Lundgate, which runs off it. The neighbourhood is full of the sights and sounds and smells of 10th century Jorvik. Townspeople are there, buying and selling, working and playing.

Open seven days a week throughout the year. From 1 April until 31 October—9 a.m. to 7 p.m. From 1 November until 31 March—9 a.m. to 5.30 p.m. Last admissions one hour before closing.

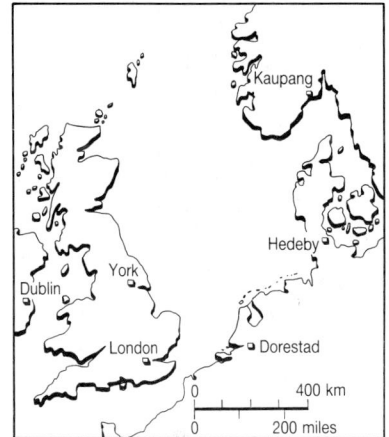

York and some other important Viking-age trading centres.

A number of publications about Jorvik and Viking York, as well as posters and gifts, are available from:
The York Archaeological Trust,
3 Kings Court,
Kings Square,
YORK YOI 2LE England

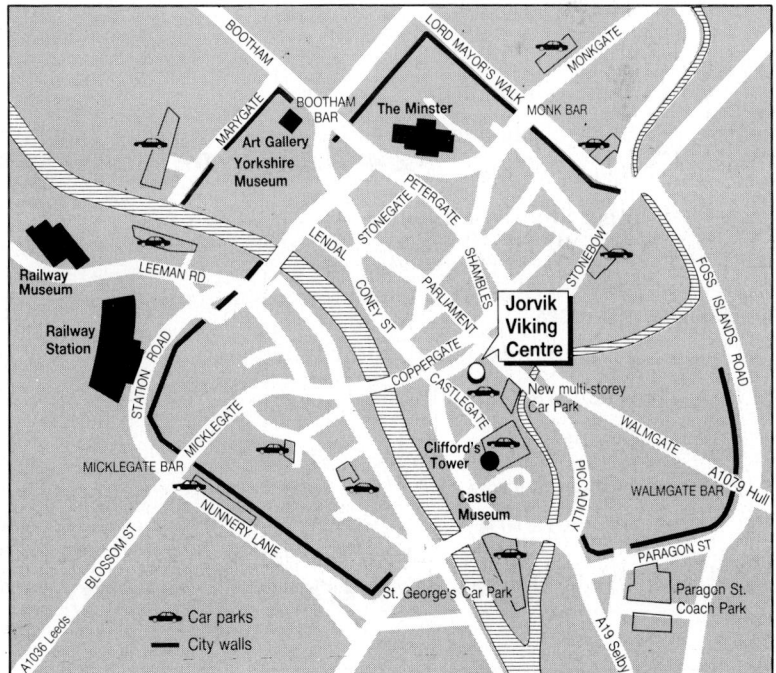

8

Lost: Dog . . .

'The Wally Phillips Show' is a popular radio programme in Chicago. Every morning listeners can phone Wally Phillips and talk to him on the radio.

One day, the Chicago Police received information about a lost dog, and they informed Larry Shriner, a reporter who works for the radio station. The police thought that radio listeners could perhaps help them. Here is the story:

1   The original facts

```
TUESDAY 29 MAY:
5.32 A.M. LARRY'S REPORT
5.33 - 6.00 A.M. WALLY'S REMINDERS TO LISTENERS
```

Task 1

You are going to hear Larry's first report on the lost dog and several examples of Wally's repetition of the information. Before listening, read the forms below carefully. In pairs, check that you understand all the vocabulary.

As you listen, fill in as much information as you can on the forms. Don't worry if you can't fill in all of the information.

LOST PROPERTY OFFICE: CANINE DIVISION

A. Description of animal

   i. name: ....

  ii. breed (see next page):..

 iii. sex (circle one):   M   F

 iv. color (circle one):   white   brown   black   other........................

  v. size: ....*24 inches from ground to shoulder*.....................

 vi. other identifying marks: ....*tattoo in right ear:*...........

vii. value $ ....

B. Circumstances

   i. On map (next page), show where animal was lost:

  ii. When was animal lost?..

 iii. Details: ....

C. Information on Owner

  name: ......*Mary*.......... ....*Adams*..........
            (first)   (middle)   (last)

  ......*Havre-de-Grace*...... ......*Maryland*......
            (city)   (state)

1 Chow

2 Beagle

3 Belgian Sheep Dog

4 Cocker Spaniel

5 Basset Hound

6 Yorkshire Terrier

7 Toy Poodle

8 Golden Retriever

9 other ....

O'Hare Airfield

CANFIELD AVE.

HARLEM AVE.

KENNEDY EXPRESSWAY

WAUKEGAN DRIVE

LINCOLN AVENUE

(6000N)

N

0   1   2   3 miles

0 1 2 3 4 5 km

CICERO AVENUE

(4500N)

NORTH AVENUE

(3000N)

EISENHOWER EXPRESSWAY

ROOSEVELT RD

DAN RYAN EXPRESSWAY

29TH STREEET

HALSTED STREET

WABASH AVENUE

(2900S)

55TH STREET

(5500S)

61ST STREET (6100S)

67TH STREET (6700S)

L a k e   M i c h i g a n

LOST PROPERTY OFFICE: CANINE DIVISION: SUPPLEMENTARY SHEET

```
┌─────────────────────────────────────────────────────────────────┐
│ MORE FACTS FROM A LISTENER: 6.05 A.M. BARBARA'S CALL              │
└─────────────────────────────────────────────────────────────────┘
```

Task 2

🖭 Barbara, a radio listener, knows a lot about the lost dog. Look at the information about three champion dogs, and then listen to the information Barbara gives.

Which one of these champions is the lost dog?

Desiree de la Pourosse
("Desi")
born: Brussels, 1980
weight: 58 lbs
🏆: Las Vegas, 1983
owner: M. L. Adams

Desiree la Belle
("Belle")
born: Maryland, 1981
weight: 70 lbs
🏆: Minneapolis, 1984
owner: M. T. Adams

Desiree Mon Amour
("Amie")
born: Minneapolis, 1980
weight: 66 lbs
🏆: (none)
owner: M. R. Adams

Compare your choice with another student's and then add any new information to the report form on pages 34 and 35.

```
┌─────────────────────────────────────────────────────────────────┐
│ TWO MORE LISTENERS CALL WALLY: 6.15 A.M. PAT'S CALL              │
│                                 6.23 A.M. BILL'S CALL            │
└─────────────────────────────────────────────────────────────────┘
```

Task 3

In pairs, read the sentences below and check that you understand all the vocabulary.

🖭 Listen to Pat's call and decide which sentences are true and which are false.

T/F

☐ Pat saw a dog on the Dan Ryan.

☐ When the woman saw the dog, she slowed down.

☐ There was an accident.

☐ This happened yesterday evening.

☐ The woman took the dog to an animal shelter.

Compare your answers with a partner's. Try to correct the false statements together.

Task 4

What do you think? Did the woman see Desiree, or was it a different dog? Use the information you have collected on pages 34 and 35 to help you decide. Give reasons for your answer.

Task 5

Listen to Bill's call and indicate on the map where he saw a dog.

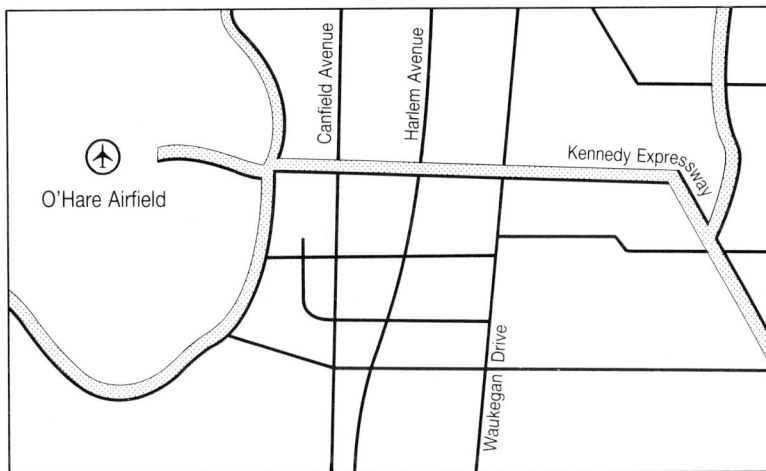

Compare your answers with a partner's and then add the information to the map on page 35.

Task 6

Listen to Bill's call again and answer these questions:

- When did he see a dog?
- Does it correspond to Desiree's description?

Task 7

What do you think? Did Bill see Desiree, or was it a different dog? Use the information you have collected on pages 34 and 35 to help you decide. Give reasons for your answer.

THE REPORTER CALLS BACK: 6.28 A.M. LARRY'S SECOND REPORT

2   Some new information

Task 1

Larry Shriner, the reporter, called again. There was a mistake in his
first report and he had some new information to give.

Listen to Larry and to Wally's comments. Can you identify the new
information?

new information?

Description of dog:	no̸/yes:	. . . .
Information about owner:	no̸/yes	. . .*3.6. years old*. . . . . .
Where dog was lost:	no/yes:	. . . .
When dog was lost:	no/yes:	. . . .

Put the new information on your police report form on page 35.

Task 2

Because of these new facts, Wally wanted to talk to one of the callers
again. In pairs, look at all the information you have and try to decide
who Wally wants to talk to.

Listen and check your answer.

ANOTHER LISTENER CALLS: 6.44 A.M. CAROLYN'S CALL

Task 3

Pat's daughter, Carolyn, called Wally to give him some more
information about what happened to her yesterday.

Read your notes on Pat's call again (Task 3, page 36) and then read
the sentences below.

Listen to Carolyn's story and decide which of the sentences below
are true and which ones are false.

Check your answers with a partner's.

T/F

☐ She was on the Dan Ryan yesterday.

☐ A dog was walking across the expressway, so she stopped.

☐ Carolyn was hurt in the accident which followed.

☐ Carolyn and her fiance took the dog to an animal shelter on 41st and Wabash.

☐ The dog corresponds to Desiree's description.

☐ The dog is still at the animal shelter.

THE LAST CALL:

Task 4

Look at this column from a Chicago telephone directory. Which of these places is Wally going to call now?

📼 Listen to check your answer.

6.48 A.M. WALLY TALKS TO BOB.

Task 5

📼 Bob has just arrived at work so he doesn't know if Desiree is at the shelter. Listen to his conversation with Wally and try to answer these questions:

When will he know if Desiree is there? . . . .

Is Bob going to call Wally back? . . . .

Task 6

Wally told the story one more time before the end of his radio programme on May 29th.

📼 Listen to his summary if you have any questions about the details of the story.

Animal Boarding Farms

See
Kennels

Animal Breeders—Fur & Laboratory

KOCH CHINCHILLA RANCH
FOR SALE
PEDIGREE RIBBON SHOW STOCK
MUTATIONS (White – Silver – Beige
Black – Charcoal & Blends)
PRIMING AND PELTING SERVICE
CHINCHILLA SUPPLIES
VISITORS BY APPOINTMENT ONLY
4708 Glenway Av **471-1947**

Animal Breeders Supplies

See Pet Shop Supplies

Animal Dealers—Pets

See Pet Shops; also Dog Kennels

Animal Hospitals

Animal Medical Clinic at Gulf Gate Inc
2316 Stickney Point Rd – **922-0756**
Cortez Animal Clinic
4224 Cortez Rd W – **756-2990**

Animal Shelters

Animal Welfare League
6124 S Wabash Av – **667-0088**
Bishop Animal Shelter
5718 21st Av W – Bradenton **792-2863**
HUMANE SOCIETY
2331 15th St **955-4131**

Animal Spray

See Insecticides & Pest Control Products

3 The whole story

Task 1

The next day a Chicago newspaper printed Desiree's story. In fact, some of the information in the newspaper article is different from the story you know. Find the details which are different.

DESIREE FINDS ADVENTURE ON THE DAN RYAN

A $25,000 Belgian sheepdog was finally returned to its owner yesterday, but only after causing several accidents on the Dan Ryan Expressway and spending the night in south Chicago.

The story began on Monday afternoon when Desiree de la Pourosse, a four-year-old prize-winner, jumped through a small window in her trailer. The dog's owner, Mary Linda Adams of Havre de Grace, MD., was taking the dog home after a show in Minneapolis. "We didn't know Desiree was missing until someone stopped us about a mile down the road," she said. "They told us they'd seen her jump out and disappear into the traffic. I was just terrified. We went back and talked to the police, and everybody began looking for her, but we couldn't find her anywhere."

They couldn't find the dog because it was already on its way to an animal shelter in south Chicago. Carolyn Schlaffer and her fiance, John Eckenfels, had caught Desiree and were taking her to the Animal Welfare League, 6124 S. Wabash Avenue. "There was lots of traffic," Eckenfels said, "and the dog was running all over the expressway. We slowed down and a car ran into us." Eckenfels caught the dog, but then a third car crashed into the two wrecked ones. A minute later there was another collision when drivers slowed down to look at the three-car crash up. "What a mess!" Ms. Schlaffer added. "The police weren't interested in the dog. They just told us to drive off the expressway and leave it somewhere. We knew it was probably someone's special pet, so we took it to the animal shelter."

On Tuesday morning, Desiree's 'disappearance' was included in the police report on WGN's Wally Phillips Show. A friend of Schlaffer's was listening and a few hours later Desiree was safely back in her trailer. "I'm so happy to have her back," Adams said.

Schlaffer was happy, too, but now she has a problem of her own. The driver of the car that hit her brand new Chevrolet didn't have any insurance for the vehicle.

TEACHER'S GUIDE

UNIT 1

1   There's a place

Task 1
This activity is meant to elicit the topic (countries, geography) from the students and it should be done with books closed.

2   Your turn

Task 1
The 'How good is your geography?' game is based on an idea in *The Puzzle Mountain* Gyles Brandreth (Penguin 1981)
NB   The country outlines are not done to scale.

3   Right or wrong?

Task 1
Steve's answers: **1** Denmark   **2** Norway
                           3 Portugal   **4** Spain   **5** Korea
                           6 India   **7** England
                           8 Argentina   **9** New Zealand
                           10 Iraq.

Task 2
Correct answers: **1** Denmark   **2** Norway
                           3 Korea   **4** Nigeria   **5** Spain
                           6 India   **7** England
                           8 Argentina   **9** New Zealand
                           10 Iraq.

UNIT 2

1   Before the trip

Task 4
1 c   2 b   3 e

Task 5
Letter **b** was sent to confirm the telephone conversation.

Task 6
Timetable **b** in Task 4 relates to letter **b** in Task 5.

2   On the spot

Task 1
Reason for moving: no more room at the hotel.

Task 2
A room is booked in conversation 4.

Task 3
Hotel Belmont: Room 406
Hotel Templer: Room 22; 720–65–06; till Thursday
Hotel Beaux Arts: in Lyon; till Sunday
Hilton Hotel: at Orly Airport; 687–33–88; till Tuesday.

3   Next stop

Task 1
Students should read the timetable before listening. You may need to answer students' queries as to the meaning of, for example: Paris (Charles de Gaulle); daily; the arrival time being the same time as the departure time (because British time is one hour behind French time and the length of the flight is one hour); etc.
1 Paris Charles de Gaulle   **2** London, Gatwick
3 5   **4** 261–50–21

Task 2
This is a good exercise to do in the language laboratory, if you have one, as students can then work individually.

Task 4
The song is 'Leaving on a Jet Plane' written by John Denver.

UNIT 3

1   Hello?

Task 1
These 'messages', left by the owners of answerphones, introduce the subject of telephone messages.

2   I'd like to leave a message . . .

Task 1
Students listen only for the names mentioned. After a first playing they can compare answers together before going on to Task 2.

Catherine   3   (messages 3, 5, 6)
Thomas   1   (message 2)
Julie   2   (messages 1, 4)

Task 2
Students read and talk about the advertisements before listening to the recorded messages from Task 1 again. Messages 1 ('flat'), 2 ('Amsterdam') and 3 ('advertisement', practise my French) are clearly in answer to advertisements.

Task 3
Because no names are mentioned, students must understand other details in the messages in order to be able to clarify them correctly.

Catherine: i, iv
Thomas: iii
Julie: ii, v.

Task 4
v is the only personal call.

Task 5

Students take notes on the business calls. This involves comprehension of spelling, numbers, days and times. Play the messages several times, with students checking their work together after each playing.

Name of caller	Reason for calling	Phone number	Best time to call back
i Andrea Gibson	wants evening classes	35–26–01–42	this evening
ii Sally Edgar	wants to start lessons on Monday afternoons	47–82–24–06	anytime
iii Jim Starkey	wants information about French courses	32–18–09–96	evenings only
iv Martha Holmes	wants an intensive French course	68–61–04–11	8–10 a.m. after 7 p.m.

3   I saw your ad ...

Task 1
As in Section 1 Task 2, students read and talk about the advertisements.

Task 2
With students in three small groups (each group choosing a different advertisement), play the messages through completely. During this first listening students count the number of messages which concern them.
During the second playing, students take notes as they did in Section 2 Task 5. Then they compare notes within their small groups and listen again if necessary.

Task 3
After exchanging notes with another group, students listen again and check the notes they have been given.

   i camera   42–86–11–12
   ii Elizabeth Barnes   car   31–46–89–04
   iii car   Mr Roper   work: 35–52–90–44 home: (after 6 p.m.) 32–46–21–21
   iv apple-picking   43–98–18–92
   v Louis de Perne   camera   all day tomorrow for appointment;   call tonight 31–46–89–99
   vi Simon   apple-picking   32–46–32–67   this evening
   vii car   before 10 a.m.   47–39–50–85   Brian
   viii Sonny Lowe   45–66–85–32   apple-picking

UNIT 4

1   A mixed bag

Tasks 1 and 2
In both of these tasks there is more than one possible answer. Some students may feel, for example, that the time announcement just before the traffic news is part of the traffic news.

2   Commercial break

Task 1
It is not necessary to teach the vocabulary for the products and services in the pictures as the radio advertisements contain several elements which can help the students to guess the product (e.g. telephone noises, telecom, telecommunicating, British Telecom, phone shop, Inphones, press button dialling, last number recall).

The advertisements are for the following:
1 used cars (Penta)
2 houses (Charles Church Homes)
3 telephones (British Telecom)
4 a classified advertisements magazine (*Finder*)
5 Alitalia airlines

Task 2
Advertisement 1
a 'At Penta we try harder to make buying a used car easier and better for you.'
b every day

Advertisement 2
a on Friday evening and Saturday all day.
b False

Advertisement 3
a £29.95
b Mondays to Fridays 9 to 5 Saturdays 9.30 to 4

Advertisement 4
a once a week
b False

Advertisement 5
a Pisa Milan Venice Rome Turin Bologna
b 3 per day.

3   Door to door

Tasks 1, 2 and 3
The advertisement is for Electrolux — sewing machines, vacuum cleaners, floor polishers, etc.

UNIT 5

1   Do you remember when ...?

Task 1
Give students time to do the matching together, but do not encourage discussion of the dates or contexts of the quotations as this will be done in Task 3.

a Winston Churchill
b Neil Armstrong
c Mohammed Ali
d Martin Luther King
e John Lennon
f John F. Kennedy
g Edward VIII

Task 2
Play the five extracts through without stopping. Students will probably be able to identify the quotations readily, after which they can check their answers together.

Task 3
1 b 2 a 3 f 4 d 5 g
In this activity, students discuss the dates and contexts of the quotations, listening again if necessary. When they have decided on their answers, refer them to page 64.

Task 4
Check students' answers before going on to Task 5.
a 4 b 3 c 1 d 5 e 2

Task 5
Extract 1
TWA bombing (2 April 1986) Key words: 'bomb', 'jet', 'TWA Boeing 727', 'sky'.
Extract 2
Chernobyl accident (28 April 1986) Key words: 'Soviet Union', 'nuclear accident', 'plant', 'Chernobyl', 'Ukraine', 'radiation'.
Extract 3
Release of Soviet dissident, Shcharansky (11 February 1986) Key words: 'Shcharansky', 'human rights', 'Soviet Union', 'Berlin'.

2   People and places

Tasks 1 and 2
Play the extracts through once or twice without stopping before asking students to share their notes. When they have agreed on the notes, they can begin guessing the events as a group.

People	Places	Other important words
the Queen the Duke of Edinburgh Prince Andrew Miss Sarah Ferguson	Windsor Buckingham Palace the United Kingdom the Commonwealth	balcony Happy Birthday
King Juan Carlos Queen Sophia Prince Charles Princess Diana the Prime Minister	Spain Windsor Castle the Houses of Parliament Downing Street Gibraltar	first state visit . . . since 1905 diplomacy EEC NATO

People	Places	Other important words
the Royal Family the Duchess of Windsor Mrs W. W. Simpson Edward VIII the Duke of Windsor David	Paris Windsor	age of 89 married 35 years Duke's death in 1972 sad, lonely old woman love affair of the century

1 Queen Elizabeth II's 60th birthday (21 April 1986)
2 State visit to London by King Juan Carlos of Spain (22 April 1986)
3 Death of the Duchess of Windsor (24 April 1986)

3   Take note
The tasks in Section 3 encourage students to use their knowledge of the world — as well as key words they have heard — to understand the content of the extracts:

Task 1
Give students time to read the words and ask any questions.

Task 2
Play the extract through once without stopping, then ask students to compare their answers. Play a second time to confirm their decisions.
All the words appear in the extract except Kiev, power station, Russia.
As a group, students re-tell the news item using the circled words. The item concerns a ban on the sale of lambs due to radiation levels.

Task 3
The purpose of this task is to give students practice in identifying key words. It is not necessary for a listener to hear and understand every word in an extract to be able to understand it. Exploit the extracts separately, using the procedure outlined in Task 2.

The events are:
1 The election of Pope John Paul II (16 October 1978)
2 Birth of the first test-tube baby (27 July 1978)
3 The Jonestown mass suicide (19 November 1978)

Task 4
This activity can be done regularly in class (or by students working alone at home) using recent news items.

UNIT 6

1   Outside

Task 1
Give students time to discuss the works together. They may know some of the works, but you should not provide names if they do not.

Task 2
Students should listen for a general idea of each discussion so as to be able to number the works in order.
1b (The Burghers of Calais) Key words: 'they', 'keys', 'these guys', 'suffering'.
2c (The Thinker) Key words: 'What's he thinking about?', 'muscles on his arms,' 'look at the size of the legs'.
3d (Balzac) Key words: 'a lump!', 'a great mass', 'that cape doesn't give him any shape at all'.
4a (The Gate of Hell) Key words: 'a door or a gate or something,' 'three figures on the top', 'What's The Thinker doing up there?'

Task 3
Students may be able to remember some of the comments/questions and match them to works. Other items may require discussion in pairs or groups before the passage is replayed for confirmation.

	Comments		Questions
c	'Maybe he's a Greek god or something.'	b	'Did they (die)?'
a	'What is it? A door or a gate or something . . .'		
b	'The city was under siege, I think. . .'		
d	'. . . and then they didn't want it after he made it . . .'		
b	'It was something about the Hundred Years' War, wasn't it? That was when it took place . . .'	d	'So it was a controversial statue, this one?'
a	'It must tell a story, mustn't it? . . . goodness knows what the story is!'	a	'What's The Thinker doing up there?'
c	'An athlete, probably, I mean . . .'	c	'What's he thinking about?'

Task 4
Students listen to the passage to decide which comments from Task 3 are, in fact, true.

	Comments	
✗	'Maybe he's a Greek god or something.'	'the poet, Dante . . . the artist who is both dreamer and creator'; 'So it isn't a god.'
✓	'What is it? A door or a gate or something . . .'	'And, it is a sort of door.' 'It's called The Gate of Hell.'
✓	'The city was under siege, I think . . .' '. . . and then they didn't want it after he made it . . .'	'. . . blockaded for eleven months.' 'They were shocked . . . and refused to accept it.'
✓	'It was something about the Hundred Years' War, wasn't it? That was when it took place . . .'	'to commemorate an event of the Hundred Years' War'; 'I had that much right . . .'
✓	'It must tell a story, mustn't it? . . . goodness knows what the story is!'	'inspired by Dante's *Inferno*'; 'the problem of life and death'
✗	'An athlete, probably. I mean . . . look at the size of the legs . . .'	'the poet, Dante . . . both dreamer and creator.'

In their discussion, the students should be able to answer the questions from Task 3:

'Did they (die)?'	'was stopped . . . by his wife the Queen'; 'Oh, they didn't die in the end.'
'So it was a controversial statue, this one?'	'refused to accept it saying it was "disrespectful" and looked like a "melting snowman"; so that was the controversy.'
'Now what's The Thinker doing up there?'	'If The Thinker is Dante, and the door is Hell, then it's, you know, Dante's *Inferno*.' 'At the top, his head on his hand, is The Thinker, pondering the problem of life and death.'
'What's he thinking about?'	'the poet, Dante, meditating upon his creation'; 'So I guess that means he's thinking about the *Inferno*'.

2 Inside

Tasks 1 and 2
These serve as an introduction to the listening task. Students should be given time to discuss their opinions and match titles, giving their reasons.

Task 3
1b (The Cathedral) Key words: 'cupping round each other', 'see right down through the middle', 'the space inside', 'open', 'finely done'.
2c (The Hand of God) Key words: 'huge hand', 'two figures', 'Adam and Eve'.
3a (The Secret) Key words: 'shorter fingers', 'box inside'.

3 What do you think?

Task 1
Again, give students time to enjoy the works and share their feelings about them.

Task 2
This listening activity involves two phases:
i determining the order of the works discussed by identifying key words, and

ii understanding each person's reaction by recognizing vocabulary of likes and dislikes.

Some students may be able to accomplish the two phases simultaneously while others may need to listen twice.

	Key words	Man	Woman
1 Idyll of Ixelles	'baby angels'	likes	likes
2 Young woman . . .	'she's lovely', 'like those girls in Renoir's paintings'	likes	dislikes
3 Torso	'only half-done' 'muscles' 'strong'	dislikes	likes
4 Cry of pain	'depressing' 'too much suffering'	dislikes	dislikes

UNIT 7

1 What shall we do?

Task 2
The extracts concern the following places/activities: exhibition, dance, motorbike race, fashion show.

Task 3
Locations:
1 London   2 Bewdley (but train travels 12½ miles therefore not limited to Bewdley   3 York
4 Windsor   5 Edenbridge   6 not stated in the ad. but students may know that the British Museum is in London.

Task 4
Advertisement 3

2 A voyage of discovery

Task 4
Trade wine   jewellery   amber
Standard of living 'They were enjoying a very comfortable standard of living, nice houses, nice things to use, good food. They would be very comfortably off by our standards.'
The first sentence has the same meaning as the one above.

Task 5
Some of the impressions which students should have are, for example:
- that it is an exciting new venture and a revolutionary concept in museum design;
- that visitors travel through the museum in special cars;
- that the Viking Centre shows life in a Viking village 1000 years ago.

Task 6
At the second playing, the teacher can pause at // if necessary:

There was so much excitement about the village buried at the heart of York that it was decided to reconstruct a whole street and *people it with life-size models of people at work.*// Visitors go round the street in small electronically-controlled *cars*// which the staff say *travel through time into the tenth century . . .*//

The extract from the guidebook should be numbered as follows:

In the Jorvik Viking Centre 1 *people from the 20th century journey back in time to the 10th century.* 2 *The journey is done in time cars*, which silently glide back through the years, past some of the thirty or so generations of York's people who have walked the pavements of Coppergate*, until time stops, on a late October day in 948. For a while modern time travellers explore Coppergate and a little alley, Lundgate, which runs off it. The neighbourhood is full of the sights and sounds and smells of 10th century Jorvik. 3 *Townspeople are there, buying and selling, working and playing.*

(* 'Coppergate' is the name of the street in which the Jorvik Viking Centre is located. Many streets in York have names ending in '-gate': Stonegate, Petergate, Coppergate. 'Gate' is from an old Norse word meaning 'street'.)

Some impressions students should now have:

- Jorvik shows the Viking as a trader rather than as the pirate and raider we often imagine him to be.
- the centre was built on the site of archaeological excavations and contains a reconstruction of the Viking village that was found there.
- the village is peopled with life-size models of Vikings at work.
- visitors to Jorvik travel backwards in time, through a time tunnel which includes the reconstructed Viking village.
- the journey is done in electronically-controlled 'time' cars.

Task 7
The scenes mentioned by Viv are, in order:
g the woodturner: 'This is the person who makes wooden bowls and things like that.'
e the shoemaker: 'Oh, it's the shoemaker . . . makes leather shoes.'
i the jeweller: 'Oh, he makes jewellery, yes.'
b hearth scene: 'This is the hearth . . .'
d loom: 'Oh, this is a loom.'
c cesspit: 'Oh, look at this. This is the cesspit . . .'
a fishing boat: 'Here's the boat coming in.'
h fishermen: 'There's two fishermen telling stories to a young boy . . .'
f archaeological dig: 'Now we're coming back to 1980. This is the archaeological excavation work.'

Task 8
The scenes mentioned by the reporter are, in order:
e 'On the left there's a bench . . .'
d 'On the right at the moment there's a loom . . .'
b 'behind me there's a domestic hearth scene . . .'
c 'Coming up on the left is the cesspit . . .'
a 'A little further we came across a fishing boat . . .'
f 'At the end of the time tunnel is a display of Viking buildings . . . frames of walls'

UNIT 8

1   The original facts

Students read the short introduction to understand the type of radio programme they will be listening to (i.e. a live programme which receives calls from listeners).

In addition to discussing the type of programme, you may wish to prepare students for Task 1 by encouraging a discussion of lost dogs, e.g. What would you do if your dog was lost? Where would you go? Who would you contact? What information would you give them? In this way, students can be sensitized to the type of information included on the forms in Task 1.

Task 1

Students must be given as much time as they need to read the forms on these two pages before listening to the tape. It can be helpful to bring the following to students' attention:

'breed': eight examples are given on the second form.
map: streets running east and west in Chicago are often
        numbered, e.g. a street which is 55 blocks south of
        the centre is called '55th Street' and is said to be
        'fifty-five hundred South' (5500 S). Streets running
        north and south are named, and houses on them are
        numbered according to the nearest east/west
        streets. I.e. houses between 55th and 56th streets
        will be numbered between 5500 and 5599.
        This information is not absolutely necessary, but it
        can help students in their listening tasks.

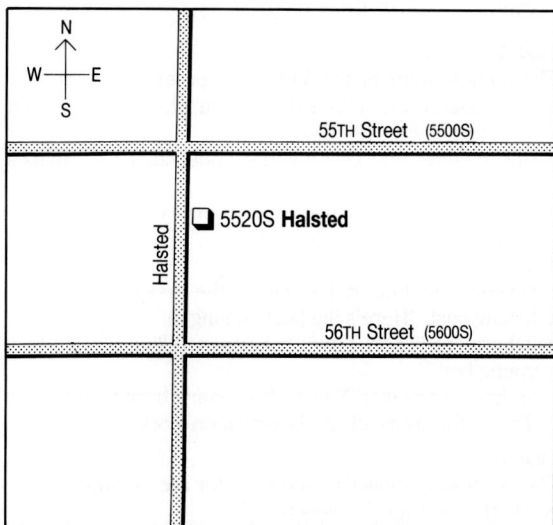

'Expressways': high speed, limited access roads. If you pronounce the names of various streets and expressways, students will find it easier to identify them while listening.

'The Original Facts' are the reporter's initial information followed by four subsequent repetitions. The times of the report and repetitions have been recorded and, with the short pauses, serve as indicators that a new segment is beginning. Before playing the tape a first time, remind students that because of the number and nature of the segments the same information is repeated many times. Also tell students that all segments will be re-played if necessary. It is very important to provide this sort of reassurance as students may initially find the speed of authentic English rather surprising.

After the complete first playing, students compare and share the information they've noted on their forms. It is not necessary to understand and note all of the information requested before going on to Task 2 as it will be repeated there. The only essential piece of information, which students must note before going on, is the fact that the dog is said to have been lost 'this morning'. The teacher must be sure that each student has written this information on the form. Do not play segments in Task 1 more than twice before going on to Task 2.

Name: Desiree
Breed: 3 (Belgian Sheepdog)
Sex: F
Color: Black
Tatoo: JRR (followed by a number)
Lost at 29th St and the Dan Ryan Expressway
* Lost this morning (this information is given in segment 3 only)
Details: jumped from owner's car

(* Essential information before going on to the next activity)

Task 2

Give students time to read the introduction and look at the photos and descriptions. The rosettes represent prizes or competitions won. Students listen and compare answers.

The first photo is correct.
New information is: 'Linda' (owner's middle name), 'prick ears' or 'ears that stand up', and 'long tail'.

All subsequent listening and discussion activities follow the procedures outlined above, i.e. students read the material provided, listen then compare their answers. They can then re-listen to check their work.

Task 3

F (Pat's daughter saw a dog.) T T F (This happened yesterday afternoon.) T.

Task 4

In fact, even though the location is exact, the dog is probably not Desiree as she was lost this morning and Pat's daughter saw a dog yesterday afternoon.

Task 5

Bill saw the dog near the Kennedy Expressway between Canfield and Harlem.

Task 6

Bill saw a dog corresponding to Desiree's description yesterday afternoon. It was several miles from 29th and the Dan Ryan, so neither the location nor the time corresponds to the facts.

2 Some new information

Task 1
New information: Desiree was lost yesterday afternoon.

Task 2
Students are expected to realize that Pat's story now corresponds to the facts.

Task 3
T T F (Carolyn said, 'No, I'm fine.') F ('61st and Wabash') T T

Task 4
Wally is going to telephone the Animal Welfare League at 61st and Wabash.

Task 5
Bob will know in half an hour, and Wally will call him back.

Task 6
An optional activity, this extract re-tells the story. Students can follow and check the information they've gathered.

3 The whole story

Task 1
According to the newspaper:
The dog jumped from a trailer, not a car.
There was a third accident.
It was a friend of Schlaffer's (not her mother) who was listening to the radio.

Additional information is provided about the dog, the circumstances of her disappearance, and the accidents which followed.

TEXT OF THE RECORDED MATERIAL

[ ] enclose language which does not appear in the recording.

* * enclose language which may not be considered correct outside its context in the recording.

( ) enclose another speaker's background comments.

'going to' is often produced as 'goin[g t]o', and this phenomenon has not been indicated in the transcripts.

UNIT 1

Section 1 Task 1 (1′ 15″)

Well, I love Greece and I'd really love to go back to Greece. It's so nice, and so warm, and the people are lovely, and I love swimming.

Er . . . Nepal. I like the . . . the purity of soul of the people there. They're the nicest, most direct, most unneurotic people that I've ever met anywhere in the world.

Gee, I don't know, I mean I like Turkey, er . . . I liked Austria, but I wasn't there long enough to really enjoy it. Switzerland, Switzerland, Switzerland was it. Yeah, I was hiking in Switzerland. Switzerland was grand.

Erm . . . Cyprus. The food was wonderful. The people were wonderful. The sun was wonderful, and the sea was wonderful. Cyprus is a lovely place.

It has to be Brazil. I was lucky enough to go there a couple of years ago. Erm . . . the thing that impressed me most of all were the people and how friendly they were.

Section 3 Task 1 (4′ 07″)

Woman Right, we've got this little game that we'd like you to play. Erm . . . it's guessing countries from the outlines.

Man Oh, that's going to be hard.

Woman Yes, yes it might be. I mean we've helped you out by giving you a choice at the bottom of the page . . .

Man Oh, yes. I see.

Woman . . . so that makes it a bit easier.

Man Oh well, that's not quite so bad then. I think I'll play.

Woman You'll have a, you'll have a go will you?

Man I'll have a go.

Woman Right. What do you think of number one, then?

Man Right, number one. Well, that's . . . that's a good one to start with because I know that one, I th. . . at least I think I do. I think that's Denmark, because there's lots of islands all over the place. I think I recognize that as Denmark.

Woman So you're going to go for Denmark?

Man Yes, go for Denmark on number one.

Woman Right. OK.

Man Now number two, that's oh . . . that's quite an odd one. It's long and thin with little islands off . . .

Woman Mmm . . .

Man . . . the left hand side, so that must be the sea side, and perhaps the land side's the other side. So, I think that's up in Scandinavia again. So I'm going to guess Norway for that one.

Woman Right, Norway.

Man Norway for number two.

Woman Right, and what do you make of number three?

Man Erm . . .

Woman Another funny shape.

Man That is a funny shape. Er . . . again I think that's [a] completely different part of the world. Don't know which is land and which is sea on that one. Let's have a look at the guesses I can have. I think I'll guess Portugal for number three.

Woman Portugal.

Man Mmm . . .

Woman Right. Yes, it could be couldn't it?

Man Could be. I'm not very sure about that one though. Now number four. Mmm . . . that's an odd shape, that's a square with a bit taken out of the bottom. It looks like it's all a . . . all a land border rather than coast because they're a funny shape for coasts. Mmm . . . no, I'm going to have to guess again. Call that one Spain. Spain I think for number four.

Woman Number four, Spain. Right.

Man Mmm . . . number five. Well, that's another difficult one. That's just a bit like the other one only upside down. Squarish, not much sea. Mmm . . . what are my choices again? No, I'll guess Korea for that one. Number five I think's Korea.

Woman Number five, Korea. OK.

Man Mmm . . . I hope they're going to get easier, those *was* quite difficult.

Woman I think they do get easier actually. (laughs)

Man Good. Ah yes, well they do actually. Number six, that . . . I think that's easy because that's like a triangle upside down. Lots of coastline, so I'm going to guess India for that one.

Woman Right.

Man India for number six. Now number seven's the best one of the lot.

Woman That shouldn't pose too many problems.

Man No, shouldn't pose too many problems there. I think number seven's England.

Woman Wow! Well, we'll see if you're right about that one.

Man Right, now they're getting hard again now. Number eight is a bit like number six, only it's thinner. Long and thin with an island off the bottom, I think that's an island. Yeah, er . . . I . . . I think that's going to be Argentina for number eight. Looks like Argentina.

Woman Right, so Argentina, number eight.

Man Mmm . . . now.

Woman And . . . oh goodness.

Man Number nine, that's easy that's a . . . that's getting further away though. That's two islands with some sea in the middle there, and a . . . and the top island looks like a, a ram's horn or something. So I'm going to say New Zealand for that one.

Woman Right. New Zealand. OK. And the last one is . . .

Man Mmm . . . you've saved the hardest till the last. Ooh . . . can't say what's sea or what's land there. It's like a, looks like a sh . . ., looks like a lion's head if you look at it at one angle. I'll guess Iraq, I think for that because I haven't had that one, that's the only reason why I chose that.

Woman Yes, that was a good guess.

Section 3 Task 2 (2′ 53″)

Woman OK. Let's have a look at the ones you got right, first of all. Erm . . . yes, you were right about Iraq.

Man Well, that was a lucky guess.

Woman That was a good guess. And of course you were right about your Denmark one that you got right away.

Man Yes, yes that was easy.

Woman And, yes you were right to go for Norway, rather than Sweden, on your number two. So that was good. Now you got the easy ones, you got England, which was number seven, and you got India which was number six, and you got Argentina . . .

Man Right.

Woman . . . which was number eight.

Man Yes.

Woman And you got New Zealand which was number nine. So that was very good.

Man Those were the easy ones. Now what about the hard ones?

Woman Well, I'm afraid you failed a bit on the squares.

Man Mmm . . . they all look the same to me, I'm afraid.

Woman (laughs) You did very well on your Iraq square, but number five . . .

Man Oh, yes.

Woman . . . which was erm . . . number five was the one that you thought was . . .

Man Korea, I said for that.

Woman . . . Korea, but in fact was Spain. I mean they are a bit similar . . .

Man . . . well, miles away.

Woman And then the other one you got wrong was number three . . .

Man Number three. Let's have a look at that.

Woman . . . which you said was Portugal and was in fact Korea. Korea is . . . is . . . is . . .

Man Oh dear, no I . . . didn't really have much of an idea with that one, that was a guess.

Woman And the other one you got wrong was number four, which you said was Spain, but in fact was Nigeria.

Man Oh dear.

Woman But in fact, I mean, how many did you get right? You got seven out of ten.

Man Well, I think my geography master might be reasonably (laughs) encouraged with that.

Woman Seven out of ten, I think that's not bad at all. I would say your geography is not bad at all, if you got seven out of ten.

Man Thank you. I . . . that was a good game. I enjoyed that.

UNIT 2

Section 1 Task 2 (1′ 55″)

Woman Pan Am.

Man Oh, hello Pan Am. Erm . . . I'm wondering what your flights are from London to San Francisco.

Woman We have one flight per day from London to San Francisco.

Man Ah . . . one a day.

Woman It departs . . . yes . . . it departs ten twenty-five a.m. . . .

Man Yeah . . .

Woman And arrives at one ten p.m. local time.

Man I see, and . . . erm . . . does that flight go from Gatwick or Heathrow?

Woman It goes from Heathrow.

Man OK, fine, erm . . . can you tell me the price of a . . . well, let's have a one-way ticket, please?

Woman A one-way ticket . . .

Man Yeah . . .

Woman . . . to San Francisco. Economy class. That's three hundred and eight pounds.

Man That's economy?

Woman Yes.

Man OK, that'll do fine. Erm . . . I'll call you back on this. Thank you very much for the information.

Woman Er . . . you don't want to make a reservation now?

Man No, I'll call you back.

Woman All right.

Man Bye bye now.

Woman Bye bye.

Man Hello, Aer Lingus.

Woman Oh, good morning. Er . . . yes . . . I'd like the departure times please of your Sunday flights from Rome to Dublin.

Man Yes, we have one flight on Sunday. It departs Rome three ten p.m. and arrives Dublin five twenty p.m. It's flight five oh three.

Woman Right, thank you. And . . . and . . . how much is a one-way ticket, in lire?

Man One-way ticket in lire? Just a moment, please. A one-way ticket in lire is seven hundred and sixty-four thousand lire.

Woman Right, thank you very much, you've been very helpful.
Man You're welcome.
Woman Goodbye.
Man Goodbye.

Section 1 Task 3 (4′ 25″)

Extract 1
Woman 1 KLM, good morning.
Woman 2 Oh, hello, I wonder if you could help me. Er . . . do you have any flights from Amsterdam to Vienna and back?
Woman 1 Yes, er . . . we have a flight every day, every morning, except on Saturdays.
Woman 2 So . . . the flight does operate on Sundays, then?
Woman 1 Yes, it does.
Woman 2 Oh, great. And what time does the flight leave, please?
Woman 1 Er . . . it leaves at eight oh five, that's flight number KL two five five, and it arrives in Vienna at nine forty-five.
Woman 2 Nine forty-five. Er . . . great. OK. And how much is a return ticket, please?
Woman 1 You want Amsterdam–Vienna return price, do you?
Woman 2 Yep, that's right.
Woman 1 Can you wait a moment?
Woman 2 Yeah, sure.
Woman 1 The price of the return ticket is fourteen hundred Dutch guilders.
Woman 2 Fourteen hundred Dutch guilders. Right, er . . . thanks very much.
Woman 1 You're very welcome. Goodbye.

Extract 2
Man 1 Hello, Luxair.
Man 2 Hello, er . . . yes. Erm . . . I'd like to know the times of er . . . Sunday flights, please, er . . . from Luxemburg to Paris.
Man 1 From Luxemburg to Paris on Sundays?
Man 2 Yes, please.
Man 1 Yes, well, at the moment we have two flights per day at weekends.
Man 2 Mmm hmm
Man 1 And, er . . . you may care to know that we have four per day on weekdays.
Man 2 Mmm hmm
Man 1 Now, the first departure time, seven forty a.m. arriving eight forty a.m., and that's er . . . flight number LG two oh one. And the second one, the evening flight, the departure time is six forty-five p.m. arriving at seven forty-five p.m. And that's flight number LG two oh three.
Man 2 Mmm hmm thanks very much. And, erm . . . what is the airport of arrival, please?
Man 1 Er . . . all arrivals are at Roissy Charles de Gaulle in Paris.

Man 2 Charles de Gaulle, Paris. And er . . . how much is a one-way ticket?
Man 1 You . . . s . . . will be wanting a sim . . . simp . . . simply a one-way ticket, would you?
Man 2 Er . . . yes, please.
Man 1 Yes, let me just check. Er . . . one way is four thousand six hundred and twenty Luxemburg francs.
Man 2 Four thousand six hundred and twenty Luxemburg th . . . er . . . francs.
Man 1 That's correct.
Man 2 Thanks very much.
Man 1 Not at all.
Man 2 Bye.
Man 1 Goodbye.

Extract 3
Woman Good morning, Scandinavian Airlines.
Man Oh, good morning. Erm . . . I wonder if you can help me. I'd like to know the departure times of flights on a Saturday from London to Stockholm, please.
Woman Yes, sir. Er . . . on Saturdays we have five flights to Stockholm. The first departs at eight fifty-five a.m. and arrives at twelve twenty p.m. Er . . . then there's the eleven forty-five a.m., which er . . . gets into Stockholm at three oh five p.m. Next, there's the two twenty-five p.m., arriving at five fifty p.m., and next the five oh five p.m., arriving at eight thirty p.m. And, finally, there's the six thirty-five p.m. flight which gets into Stockholm at nine fifty-five p.m.
Man Nine fifty-five. Erm . . . are all the flights from Heathrow?
Woman Er . . . yes all of them except for the five oh five p.m. flight which departs from Gatwick. The eight fifty-five, two twenty-five and five oh five flights are all British Airways flights, and the other two are Scandinavian Airlines.
Man That's fine. Erm . . . now if you could just tell me the price of a one-way ticket, please?
Woman Yes, sir. A one-way ticket is two hundred and sixteen pounds each way.
Man Two hundred and sixteen each way. That's fine. Thank you very much indeed. Goodbye.
Woman You're welcome, sir. Goodbye.

Section 1 Task 5 (1′ 40″)

Woman 1 *Allô, Bonjour, Hotel Belmont.*
Woman 2 Hello, is that the Hotel Belmont?
Woman 1 Er . . . yes.
Woman 2 Good, erm . . . I'd like a single room with bath, please, for this coming Sunday night.
Woman 1 Er . . . yes, one minute, please. Yes, Sunday. How many nights?
Woman 2 Er . . . just Sunday. Possibly one more night. Don't know yet.
Woman 1 Erm . . . for one person?
Woman 2 Er . . . yes, please.
Woman 1 Er . . . yes, that's all right. Er . . . what name?
Woman 2 It's for a Mister Lakes. I'll spell that for you. It's Mister Lakes, L-A-K-E-S.

Woman 1 Yes, can you, er . . . write er . . . to confirm, please?

Woman 2 You'd like written confirmation? Yes, certainly, no problem. Erm . . . could you tell me the price of the er . . . room with bath, please?

Woman 1 Yes, for one night four hundred and fifty-eight francs, with twenty-four francs for breakfast.

Woman 2 Twenty-four, good, that's fine. And er . . . could I just check the address, please?

Woman 1 Er . . . yes, Hotel Belmont, thirty rue Bassanno . . .

Woman 2 Er . . . could you spell that, please?

Woman 1 Er . . . B-A-S-S-A-N-N-O.

Woman 2 Thank you.

Woman 1 Paris, seven five zero one six.

Woman 2 That's Paris seven five oh one six.

Woman 1 Yes.

Woman 2 Good. Thank you very much. Goodbye.

Woman 1 Goodbye, *Madame.*

Section 1 Task 7 (1′ 00″)

Hi, erm . . . I'm in Luxemburg and I'll be in Paris this evening. I thought I'd give you a call and let you know I was coming into town. Erm . . . I'll call you probably later on tonight or in the morning. I'll be staying at the Hotel Belmont tonight and that's on the rue de Bassanno or Bassanno. OK. (laughs) Can't wait to see you. Bye, bye.

It is I, er . . . calling again. I'm still in Luxemburg. I'm leaving at six forty-five and I arrive at er . . . seven forty-five on Luxair. Erm . . . I'll tell you what, erm . . . hey . . . I . . . I'll give you a call a little later. I'll need some information on subways and that sort of thing. Oh . . . er . . . oh . . . I may just take a taxi. Anyway, I'll call you later. Take it easy.

Section 2 Task 1 (1′ 05″)

It is I again. Looks like I've caught you out of town. Erm . . . this is Monday about er . . . eleven thirty in the morning. Look I'll try to call you back later today. I'll be at the Belmont again tonight. Looks as though I've got to move out tomorrow, er . . . they don't have room. So er . . . I'll give you a call later kiddo. Bye, bye now.

This is Gary Lakes calling. It's now Monday about eight p.m. I just met with Peter Wiggins who's just told me that Pierre is out of town. Perhaps you went with him. That's why you're still not at home. (laughs) But erm . . . I'll er . . . call back again. I'm still at the Hotel Belmont, but I don't know if I can stay tomorrow. Er . . . the town's full, but they're trying to find me another hotel. So, er . . . *adieu.*

Section 2 Task 2 (2′ 55″)

Extract 1

Woman 1 *Allô, bonjour?*

Woman 2 Oh, hello. I wonder if you have a erm . . . room free for tonight, please?

Woman 1 Tonight? Er . . . no, I'm sorry, we are fully booked.

Woman 2 Oh, you have no vacancies at all for tonight?

Woman 1 No, I'm sorry.

Woman 2 Oh, well, thank you very much. Goodbye.

Woman 1 That's all right. Goodbye.

Extract 2

Man *Allô, j'écoute.*

Woman Hello, erm . . . I wonder if you had a vacancy for tonight, please?

Man *Comment?*

Woman I'm sorry, do you speak English?

Man *Ah. Je [ne] comprends rien du tout. Vous dîtes, Madame?*

Woman Oh, I'm sorry. You don't speak English at all?

Man English? *Non . . . non . . . non . . . , je te . . . je . . . je ne parle pas anglais.*

Woman Uh huh . . . I'm sorry to bother you. Thank you. Goodbye.

Man *Je . . . vous en prie. Au revoir.*

Extract 3

Man *Allô, j'écoute.*

Woman Hello, erm . . . do you speak English?

Man *Pardon?* Er . . . oh . . . oh . . . er . . . yes . . . a . . . a little.

Woman Er . . . thank you. Erm . . . could I please have a single room with bath for er . . . for tonight, please?

Man Er . . . for tonight?

Woman Yes . . .

Man . . . No, I . . . I regret, er . . . the hotel is fully booked.

Woman Oh . . . you've got no vacancies at all?

Man Er . . . no . . . no . . . I regret.

Woman Oh, all right. Thank you very much. Goodbye.

Man *Au . . . au revoir, Madame.*

Extract 4

Woman 1 *Allô, oui?*

Woman 2 Oh . . . erm . . . Hello, do you speak English?

Woman 1 Erm . . . a little.

Woman 2 Er . . . good. I'd like a single room with bath for tonight, please. Is that possible?

Woman 1 Tonight?

Woman 2 Yes.

Woman 1 One person?

Woman 2 Yes.

Woman 1 Er . . . yes. Yes, we have.

Woman 2 Good, thank you. It's for a Mister Lakes.

Woman 1 Legs?

Woman 2 I'll spell it for you. Mister Lakes, L-A-K-E-S.

Woman 1 Yes.

Woman 2 And he'll be arriving at about eight o'clock.

Woman 1 Eight o'clock?

Woman 2 That's it.

Woman 1 Er . . . thank you.

Woman 2 All right. Thank you. Goodbye.

Woman 1 Goodbye.

Section 2 Task 3 (1′ 55″)

Hello, this is I again. I've finally reached the Hotel Belmont on rue de Bassanno. Yeah . . . it's about nine o'clock and I'll probably be going to bed in a little while, I'm sort of tired. Erm . . . either give me a call in the morning, or I'll give you a call. Take it easy. Oh, er . . .

erm . . . I'm in room, oh God, what's the room number? Yeah . . . I'm in room four zero six. Goodnight.

I'm getting to know your machine very well. I'm now at the Hotel Templer. Telephone is seven two zero six five zero five. I'm in room twenty-two, and I should be here right up, er . . . through Tue. . . Thursday at noon. If you get in before then, well, if you get in give me a call.

Hello. It's me again. I'm in Lyon at the Hotel Beaux Arts. I'm coming back to Paris er . . . let's see, on Sunday. It looks like you're still out, probably, I don't know where, but I just wanted to call and I'll give you a call back again on Sunday. Thank you.

Hello, here's I again. I'm now at the Hilton at Orly airport. The number is six eight seven three three eight eight. And I'll be here probably right through Tuesday at noon. Bye, bye.

Section 3 Task 2 (1′ 18″)

. . . .

Woman Hello, er . . . I'd like some information about flights to London, please. Er . . . that's Paris to London next Tuesday, erm . . . about midday.

. . . .

Woman And what time does that get in, please?

. . . .

Woman Right. Are there any other flights after that twelve noon one?

. . . .

Woman Mmm . . . yep. Erm . . . what's the flight number of the a . . . twelve noon flight, please?

. . . .

Woman Eight eight five. Good. And er . . . what airport does it depart from, please?

. . . .

Woman Good. And what is the phone number for reservations, please?

. . . .

Woman Right. I'll call back then, thank you.

. . . .

Woman Thanks very much. Goodbye.

. . . .

Section 3 Task 3 (1′ 15″)

Man British Caledonian?

Woman Hello, er . . . I'd like some information about flights to London, please. Er . . . that's Paris to London next Tuesday, erm . . . about midday.

Man Certainly madam. Erm . . . let's see, we have a flight at noon.

Woman And what time does that get in, please?

Man Erm . . . it arrives at Gatwick twelve noon, local time.

Woman Right. Are there any other flights after that twelve noon one?

Man Er . . . let me see. Yes, the next flight is at five thirty.

Woman Mmm . . . yep. Erm . . . what's the flight number of the a . . . twelve noon flight, please?

Man Flight number eight eight five.

Woman Eight eight five. Good. And er . . . what airport does it depart from, please?

Man Er . . . from Charles de Gaulle.

Woman Good. And what is the phone number for reservations, please?

Man Er . . . it's the same as you've just called, madam.

Woman Right. I'll call back then, thank you.

Man OK.

Woman Thanks very much. Goodbye.

Man You're welcome. Bye, bye.

Section 3 Task 4 (3′ 50″)
Leaving on a jet plane (John Denver)

All my bags are packed, I'm ready to go
I'm standing here outside your door.
I hate to wake you up to say goodbye.
But the dawn is breaking, it's early morn'
The taxi's waiting, he's blowing his horn
Already I'm so lonesome I could cry.

So kiss me and smile for me.
Tell me that you'll wait for me.
Hold me like you'll never let me go.
'Cause I'm leaving on a jet plane,
Don't know when I'll be back again.
Oh babe, I hate to go.

There's so many times I've let you down
So many times I've played around.
I tell you now, they don't mean a thing.
Every place I go, I'll think of you.
Every song I sing, I'll sing for you.
When I come back, I'll wear your wedding ring.

Well, now the time has come to leave you.
One more time, please let me kiss you.
Then close your eyes and I'll be on my way.
Dream about the days to come
When I won't have to leave you alone
About the times I won't have to say:

CASSETTE 1: SIDE 2
UNIT 3

Section 1 Task 1 (0′ 55″)
Hello, this is oh seven three five seven three four three. Neither Steve or Liz Hunter are able to come to the 'phone at the moment, but if you would like to leave your name and 'phone number we'll ring you back as soon as possible. Thank you.

Hello, this is seven two four oh seven three two. Peter Payne Associates. I'm afraid there's no one in the office to take your call at the moment, but if you'd like to leave a message we'll ring you back just as soon as we return. Thank you.

Section 2 Tasks 1 and 2 (2′ 35″)

Er . . . hello. Erm . . . my name's Louise. Erm . . . I want to leave a message for Julie. Erm . . . I'm interested in the flat that you've got advertised. Erm . . . my telephone number is six five eight two four three nine seven. Erm . . . you can reach me at home in the evenings, after eight o'clock. Thank you.

Ah . . . hello. Er . . . yes, I'd like to leave a message for Thomas regarding his advertisement er . . . asking for somebody to share car expenses on a trip to Amsterdam. Er . . . my name is Patrick. Er . . . I'm an art student. Er . . . and I'm very interested in . . . in going to Amsterdam on Friday. I just want to check up on a . . . a couple of details, like er . . . what time you'll be leaving. Now er . . . unfortunately you can't ring me back because I'm staying in a hotel. So I'll 'phone back in a couple of hours. OK, thanks very much. Goodbye.

Oh, erm . . . I'd like to leave a message for Catherine, please. I've read your advertisement. Er . . . my name is Mary Lucas, and I'd like to practise my French. Now my telephone number is three nine two nine four one double six. And er . . . you could 'phone me er . . . between eight in the morning and ten o'clock at night, er . . . any day at all. Thank you. Goodbye.

Oh, hello, er . . . I was hoping to speak to Julie. Erm . . . er . . . er . . . well, I haven't got a 'phone so I'll have to call her back. Erm . . . that's all.

Hello, Catherine. It's Bill. Surprise, surprise! Look, I'm just over for the Paris Motor Show. If you want to share a bottle of wine, give us a ring. All right? Four two six oh three two six oh. Cheers.

Oh, er . . . hello Catherine. It's Anne. Erm . . . listen I'm going down to spend a week with John and Caroline, so I'll give you a call when I get back. OK. Bye.

Section 2 Task 3 (2′ 23″)

Yeah, hi, my name is John Henderson. Now, I've just read your ad about the French lessons and er . . . I'd like to er . . . pursue my work in French, and er . . . I would appreciate it if you could call me. My number is er . . . three two five six nine seven three oh. That's during the days, or at . . . at night you can get me at four three two oh one two one six. Thank you very much.

Oh, er . . . er . . . I'm calling on behalf of er . . . Paula Ryan who . . . who saw your advertisement. Er . . . she's looking for a flat and . . . and she'd like to know more about the one in your advertisement. Erm . . . could you call her back, please? Er . . . her number is four two eight three oh four eight one. Thank you.

Hello, my name is Bob Carson, and my number is six five zero one er . . . four eight eight eight. Now erm . . . I'm just wondering if you have room for two of us, myself and my friend, on your trip to Amsterdam. If you have, could you call me back, please? Thank you very much.

Oh, hello, my name's Linda Brown. I saw your advertisement, erm . . . about giving conversation classes. I would very much like some French conversation classes, so perhaps you could ring me. Er . . . my number is four one seven five eight oh two two. That's four one seven five eight oh two two. Thank you very much. End of message.

Oh yes, hello, my name is Graham Roberts. Er . . . my wife and I are looking for an apartment to rent for approximately three months. Erm . . . I wonder if you could possibly let me have a few more details about the one you mention in your advertisement. If you'd be so kind as to telephone me, my number is four seven two two five oh eight six. Many thanks.

Section 2 Tasks 4 and 5 (2′ 13″)

Oh, er . . . hello. Er . . . my name's Andrea Gibson, and I phoned you yesterday. Erm . . . I'm going to be working for the next three weeks, so I'd like to change my classes. Erm . . . to the evenings, please. So perhaps you could give me a ring this evening at home. Er . . . my number is three five two six oh one four two. Thanks.

Hello, erm . . . it's Sally Edgar here. Erm . . . this is a message for Catherine. I'd very much like to start lessons again on Monday afternoons. Erm . . . could you call me, Catherine? My 'phone number's four seven eight two two four oh six. You can 'phone me any time. All right? Bye, bye.

Hello Catherine, it's Jim Starkey here. That's S-T-A-R-K-E-Y. Er . . . I was calling to see if I could get some information about the French courses. Erm . . . could you call me back perhaps? My number's er . . . three two one eight oh nine nine six. Er . . . but I'm only there in the evenings. Thank you.

Erm . . . this is Martha Holmes, H-O-L-M-E-S. Erm . . . I wondered, I . . . I wanted to do a French course, er . . . the intensive French course you advertise, because I'm starting a job soon that er . . . needs French. Erm . . . my telephone number is six eight six one oh four double one. Er . . . and I can be reached in the morning between eight a.m. and ten. Or in the evening after seven. Is that all right?

Oh, er . . . hello, Catherine. It's me here just phoning to see if you're feeling any better, and if there is anything you need. Erm . . . I'll call you again later. Bye.

Section 3 Tasks 2 and 3 (4′ 27″)

Number 1

Oh, erm . . . hello. I've just seen your notice about the camera. Erm . . . I don't really know anything about this particular model, but if it really is cheap, could you call me back on four two eight six double one one two. Thank you.

Number 2

Hello, er . . . my name is Elizabeth Barnes, B-A-R-N-E-S. I . . . I saw your advertisement for your Peugeot, and I would be very interested in it, if you could possibly give me a ring. Er . . . my number is three one four six eight nine oh four. That's three one four six eight nine oh four. Thank you very much.

Number 3

Er . . . yes, I'm er . . . ringing about the er . . . Peugeot one oh four er . . . advertised for sale. I'm er . . . definitely interested so er . . . if you'd like to get back to me. Er . . . the name is Roper, R-O-P-E-R, and you can call me er . . . er . . . my work number is three five five two nine oh double four. Or I shall be home er . . . after six o'clock on three two four six two one two one. Thank you.

Number 4

Er . . . hello. Erm . . . I'm ringing about your apple-picking weekend. Erm . . . I'd like to know a little bit more about the arrangements, please. Erm . . . er . . . wh. . . what facilities have you for sleeping and toilet and all that? And er . . . er . . . er . . . do you have transport, are you picking us up? And er . . . well that's all really. If . . . if you wouldn't mind calling me back er . . . on er . . . forty-three nine eight one eight eight tw. . . er . . . no, wait a minute, it's four three nine eight er . . . one eight nine two. OK? That's where I'm lodging. (laughs) Bye.

Number 5

Er . . . hello, my name is Louis de Perne. I should like to make er . . . an appointment to see the Canon camera erm . . . you're advertising. Erm . . . I shall be free all day tomorrow. If the camera is still available would you please call me tonight on the following number, three one four six eight nine nine nine. Thank you.

Number 6

Hello, er . . . my name is Simon, and er . . . I'm interested in your ad about apple-picking. My number is three two four six three two six seven. Er . . . and I'll be in this evening. Thanks very much, bye.

Number 7

Er . . . hello, er . . . I'm 'phoning up about the advert for the Peugeot one oh four. Yeah . . . is . . . it still for sale? Oh blimey. Look . . . er . . . could you just ring me back, please, before ten a.m. on four seven three nine five oh eight five, and ask for Brian.

Number 8

Hi, my name is Sonny Lowe. S-O-N-N-Y L-O-W-E, and I'm at four five six six eight five three two. And I would appreciate a call, please. Erm . . . I'm extremely interested in coming out to do some apple-picking, and er . . . if you could call me at four five six six eight five three two, I'd be very grateful. Thank you.

UNIT 4

Section 1 Tasks 1 and 2 (4' 02")

'You'll do a great deal better at Penta . . .'
At Penta we try harder to make buying a used car easier and better for you. Like the Penta five hundred pound choice. We'll give you a five hundred pound discount off the car you're buying, or five hundred pounds in addition to your part-exchange price, or a five hundred pound cheque when you take delivery. It's your choice, and remember, all Penta's used cars are covered by our

unique Penta promise, and the chance to exchange within seven days.
'You'll do a great deal better at Penta'
Penta for used cars. Open seven days a week.

Charles Church, builders of quality houses, invite you to the cheese and wine opening of their third show house, The Frencham, at Mill Grange, Calcott, from six till eight p.m. Friday the fifteenth of June, and nine till five on Saturday the sixteenth. Come along and join us for cheese and wine. View this attractive three-bedroomed linked detached house and see the other two furnished luxury show houses. Decide which is the best Charles Church home for you at Mill Grange, just off Mill Lane on the A4 opposite the Calcott Golf Club. Charles Church, quality homes of character.

Twenty-three past one o'clock, Monday lunchtime. Hope you had a good weekend, by the way. Only two days, but I hope you made the most of it.
'Telecom . . . Telecom . . . Telecom . . . Telecommunicating . . .'

Get down to the British Telecom 'phone shop in Friar Street, Reading, where you'll find a great choice of in-phones, including 'Slimtel', the one-piece in-phone with press-button dialling, last-number-recall and a style you'll like for just twenty-nine ninety-five. See 'Slimtel' at the British Telecom 'phone shop. Now open at Friar Street, Reading, nine to five weekdays, and Saturdays nine thirty till four.
'Telecom . . .'

Local travel agents who've been besieged by holiday-makers looking for bargains on sale this morning, say it's getting in the way of normal business. People began queueing outside the shops early this morning, and some stood in line overnight, hoping to be among the lucky few to get the cheap tickets.

It is twenty-one minutes before nine. Bit of a hold-up as usual on the elevated section of the M4, tailing back there to Heston Services almost. But apart from that, locally things are running well on the motorways, and apart from the usual hold-ups with the long-term roadworks you shouldn't encounter any problems. Public transport OK.

Brown Chesterfield suite, sixty pounds.
Dragon 3Z computer, a hundred and thirty pounds.
McClaron Europa pram buggy, sixty-five pounds.
Boosey and Hawkes clarinet, a hundred pounds.
Pianola circa nineteen hundred, a hundred and fifty pounds.

Looking for a bargain, you're sure to find it in Finder, your weekly magazine packed with homes, jobs, motors, and hundreds of bargains. And remember, your private ads for items under a hundred pounds we'll advertise free. Finder every Friday, just twenty pence.
'Find it fast in Finder.'

Staying mostly cloudy today, with some dampness in the air, and any brightness will be limited to areas well away from the coast. Light to moderate winds from the north east will keep coastal districts very cool, at around eleven degrees Celsius, fifty-two degrees Fahrenheit, but areas well inland can expect two or three degrees more. The cloud will persist overnight with some mist and drizzle likely at times, and temperatures falling to eight degrees Celsius, sixty-four degrees Fahrenheit.

Alitalia is Italy. With three daily flights to Milan, twice daily to Rome. Throughout the week to Venice, Pisa, Turin or Bologna. All from Heathrow, all at convenient times. With superbly designed comfortable seats, a choice of great Italian wines with meals, and our in-flight duty-free boutique carrying exclusive top-class Italian merchandise, making Euro-business Alitalia the executive's choice. Alitalia, *elegante*, Alitalia.

Section 2 Tasks 1 and 2 (3′ 17″)

Number 1
At Penta we try harder to make buying a used car easier and better for you. Like the Penta five hundred pound choice. We'll give you a five hundred pound discount off the car you're buying, or five hundred pounds in addition to your part-exchange price, or a five hundred pound cheque when you take delivery. It's your choice, and remember, all Penta's used cars are covered by our unique Penta promise, and the chance to exchange within seven days.
'You'll do a great deal better at Penta.'
Penta for used cars. Open seven days a week.

Number 2
Charles Church, builders of quality houses, invite you to the cheese and wine opening of their third show house, The Frencham, at Mill Grange, Calcott, from six till eight p.m. Friday the fifteenth of June, and nine till five on Saturday the sixteenth. Come along and join us for cheese and wine. View this attractive three-bedroomed linked detached house and see the other two furnished luxury show houses. Decide which is the best Charles Church home for you at Mill Grange, just off Mill Lane on the A4 opposite the Calcott Golf Club. Charles Church, quality homes of character.

Number 3
'Telecom . . . Telecom . . . Telecom . . .
Telecommunicating . . .'
Get down to the British Telecom 'phone shop in Friar Street, Reading where you'll find a great choice of in-phones, including 'Slimtel', the one-piece in-phone with press button dialling, last number recall and a style you'll like for just twenty-nine ninety-five. See 'Slimtel' at the British Telecom 'phone shop. Now open at Friar Street, Reading, nine to five weekdays, and Saturdays nine thirty till four.

'Telecom . . .'

Number 4
Brown Chesterfield suite, sixty pounds.
Dragon 3Z computer, a hundred and thirty pounds.
McClaron Europa pram buggy, sixty-five pounds.
Boosey and Hawkes clarinet, a hundred pounds.

Pianola circa nineteen hundred, a hundred and fifty pounds.

Looking for a bargain? You're sure to find it in Finder, your weekly magazine packed with homes, jobs, motors and hundreds of bargains. And remember your private ads for items under a hundred pounds we'll advertise free. Finder every Friday, just twenty pence.
'Find it fast in Finder'

Number 5
Alitalia is Italy. With three daily flights to Milan, twice daily to Rome. Throughout the week to Venice, Pisa, Turin or Bologna. All from Heathrow, all at convenient times. With superbly designed comfortable seats, a choice of great Italian wines with meals, and our in-flight duty-free boutique carrying exclusive top-class Italian merchandise, making Euro-business Alitalia the executive's choice.
Alitalia, *elegante*, Alitalia.

Section 3 Task 1 (0′ 25″)
. . . it is the best to buy.
Let's not talk, instead I'll show you why.
But how, how can I make this clear
With you in there and me out here?
I'm gonna knock on your door,
Ring on your bell,
Tap on your window too.
Come on and open your door so I can show you more,
I'm gonna knock and ring and tap until you do.

Section 3 Task 2 (0′ 15″)
I'm gonna vacuum your floor,
Polish your hall, shampoo your carpet too.
I'm gonna show you how to get a unit now and
you will say you want to have one for you.

Section 3 Task 3 (0′ 37″)
Electrolux has the world's first computerized sewing machine that even writes! Call 4462488.

Electrolux! It is the best to buy.
Let's not talk, instead I'll show you why.
But how, how can I make this clear
With you in there and me out here?

CASSETTE 2: SIDE 1
UNIT 5

Section 1 Task 2 (3′ 20″)

Extract 1
Man 1 OK Houston I'm on the porch.
Man 2 Roger, Neil.
I'm uh . . . at the foot of the ladder. The LEM foot pads are only uh . . . uh . . . depressed in the surface about uh . . . one or two inches. . . . although the surface appears to be uh . . . very, very fine grained as you get close to it, it's almost like a powder. And, I'll step off the LEM now. That's one small step for [a] man, one giant leap for mankind.

Extract 2
From Stettin in the Baltic to Trieste in the Adriatic, an iron curtain has descended across the continent. Behind

that line lie all the capitals of the ancient states of central and eastern Europe. Warsaw, Berlin, Prague, Vienna, Budapest, Belgrade, Bucharest and Sofia. All these famous cities, and the populations around them, lie in what I must call the Soviet sphere.

Extract 3

The energy, the faith, the devotion which we bring to this endeavour, will light our country and all who serve it. And the glow from that fire can truly light the world. And so my fellow Americans, ask not what your country can do for you, ask what you can do for your country.

Extract 4

I have a dream. That my four little children will one day live in a nation where they will not be judged by the color of their skin, but by the content of their character.

Extract 5

At long last I am able to say a few words of my own. I have never wanted to withhold anything. But until now it has not been constitutionally possible for me to speak. But you must believe me when I tell you that I have found it impossible to carry the heavy burden of responsibility and to discharge my duties as King as I would wish to do without the help and support of the woman I love.

Section 1 Task 5 (1′ 20″)

Extract 1

Good evening. At least four people are now known to have been killed by a bomb on an American airliner approaching Athens airport from Rome today. A man, two women and a baby girl were sucked out of the jet — a TWA Boeing 727 — through a hole blasted in its side. They fell about 12,000 feet. A Greek shepherd saw them tumbling from the sky.

Extract 2

Good evening. The Soviet Union said tonight there's been a serious nuclear accident at one of its plants. It said there had been 'some casualties'. It's not known how many or how badly hurt they are. The leak happened at the Chernobyl nuclear plant in the Ukraine and by this evening its radiation had been recorded in Sweden, Finland, Denmark and Norway. Although higher than normal, the radiation was said to be harmless to people.

Extract 3

Good evening. Mr Anatolyi Shcharansky, the human rights campaigner, released by the Soviet Union in Berlin this morning is in Jerusalem tonight with his wife. Mr Shcharansky was escorted this morning across the Glienicke Bridge by two American ambassadors to emphasize that he was not part of the exchange of spies that then followed. Hopes built up in Washington—and partly in London—tonight that better relations could now lead towards a nuclear arms reduction in Europe.

Section 2 Task 1 (2′ 41″)

'Independent Radio News'
'And today, the sixtieth birthday of the Queen. It's been a busy and a happy one for her. This morning she attended a Thanksgiving service at Windsor, this afternoon 6,000 children wished her a happy birthday in song at

Buckingham Palace'
'our court correspondent, Dickie Arbiter'
It's never been seen before. They came from the four corners of the United Kingdom and the Commonwealth, all six thousand of them, each clutching twenty daffodils. And when the Queen appeared on the balcony, flanked by the Duke of Edinburgh, Prince Andrew and Miss Sarah Ferguson, they cheered and the ground became a carpet of yellow. For after the formality of this morning's service, it was the Nation's way of saying 'Happy Birthday Your Majesty'.
Dickie Arbiter, IRN, Buckingham Palace.

King Juan Carlos and Queen Sophia of Spain will be guests at a royal banquet at Windsor Castle tonight. The royal couple arrived on a four-day State visit today. They were greeted by Prince Charles and Princess Diana. Dickie Arbiter reports:

'This is the first State visit by a Spanish sovereign since nineteen hundred and five, and while that one was largely ceremonial, this one will get down to the serious business of diplomacy tomorrow, for that's when King Juan Carlos speaks to both Houses of Parliament, the first time a visiting sovereign has done so. Afterwards he has talks and lunch with the Prime Minister at Downing Street, and high on the agenda is likely to be Spain's role in the EEC, her recent referendum to stay in NATO, and, of course, Gibraltar.'
Dickie Arbiter, IRN, Windsor.

The Duchess, whose passion cost an English King his crown, is being recognized by the Royal Family in death in a way they always refused when she was alive. The Duchess of Windsor, the former Mrs Simpson, died at her home near Paris of pneumonia, at the age of eighty-nine. Flags will fly at half-mast when she's buried next Tuesday among royalty at Windsor. Here's our court correspondent, Dicky Arbiter:

'It was the Duchess's love affair with King Edward the eighth that forced the King to choose between the crown and his heart. It was chance that they met, it was against all odds that they should fall in love, and unprecedented that he should abdicate the throne to marry her.

And I want you to know that the decision I have made has been mine and mine alone.

They were married for thirty-five years, living in exile, just outside Paris, and the Duchess never really got over the shock of the Duke's death in 1972. In recent years she was bedridden and friends described her as a sad, lonely old woman with only her memories. It had been called the love affair of the century, and now, in death, the Duke of Windsor's final wish is to be granted, for the former Mrs Wallis Wallfield Simpson, Duchess of Windsor, will rejoin her beloved David when she's buried next to him in the Royal Family's private burial ground at Windsor.'

Section 3 Task 2 (0′ 43″)

The Northern lambs who've eaten too much radiation. Good evening. Hill farmers in the Lake District and North

Wales have been told they can't sell their lambs because of contamination from the Chernobyl nuclear accident in the Soviet Union. One lamb was found to have four times too much radioactive cesium 137. The ban on the movement and slaughter of sheep is on a thousand flocks in Cumbria and 4000 in Anglesey and Snowdonia, about a million and a quarter sheep altogether. It lasts for three weeks; the Manx government has announced a similar ban. The Agriculture Minister, Mr Michael Jopling said any lamb in the shops already was safe.

Section 3 Task 3 (2′ 50″)

Extract 1

It has been a year of surprises in Rome, but surely none was bigger than the one on Monday when the cardinals of the Roman Catholic Church elected the first non-Italian Pope in 455 years. Many names were discussed, but almost no one guessed it right when Cardinal Pericle Felice stepped out onto the balcony to announce that 58-year-old Cardinal Karol Wojtyla of Poland had been elected Pope John Paul the second. Wojtyla is the first Polish pope ever to rule the Vatican and the first from a Communist country. When the new Pope emerged onto the balcony, the Italian crowd was reserved for a moment. But when he asked them in Italian to correct his mistakes in their language and to pray for him he soon had everyone in St Peter's Square cheering.

Extract 2

It was just before midnight on Tuesday that the world's first test-tube baby was born at the hospital in Oldham in north west England. Doctors Patrick Steptoe and Robert Edwards had been working for ten years on the problem of helping women who could not conceive in the normal way to have children. They had lost count of the number of times they had removed an egg from the woman's womb, fertilized it in a laboratory with her husband's sperm, and then re-implanted it in the mother only to see it rejected. But nine months ago they tried again with Mrs Lesley Brown, and this time everything went right. Nine months later, in the maternity block at Oldham Hospital, the doctors delivered Mrs Brown's five pound twelve ounce daughter Louise, the first child to be conceived in a laboratory. In the words of Dr Edwards, she was beautiful when he last saw her as an eight-cell embryo and she's beautiful now.

Extract 3

The place was a commune called Jonestown in the jungles of Guyana in South America. A party led by Congressman Leo Ryan of California had just left, taking with it members of an American cult called the People's Temple who had wanted to defect. Ryan and four of the others were murdered before they could lift off from a nearby airfield, and back in Jonestown the leader of the cult, Jim Jones, had additional plans. Tim Carter was one of the few people there still alive to tell us about it:

'Jones told the people there that everyone would commit suicide. I saw mothers kneeling down holding their babies, and people crying, and, uh, I saw my wife holding my son who was dead . . .'

The final toll: over 900 people dead.

UNIT 6

Section 1 Tasks 2 and 3 (4′ 23″)

Man [I] tell you what—before we go inside shall we have a look round the gardens?
  (Yes.)
  There's a lot of statues out here I'd like to have a look at. (It's so nice here.)
Woman Mmm.
Man Let's er, let's go over here. Now what's that one? That's, that's The Burghers of Calais, isn't it?
Woman Yeah. There's one of, they, they have one in, near Parliament, in London. A, a cast of the same statue.
Man Yeah, er, now The Burghers of Calais. That was something to do with, was it, they they were pre-preventing the king from taking over Calais by giving him the keys of the town. Wasn't that it?
Woman The city was under siege, I think (Yes) and they were all starving to death so instead of everybody dying the city elders, who were these guys, said that they would sacrifice themselves. (Gave them)
Man Right. So they they got the keys to the city and they sacrificed themselves.
Woman They said 'Take us and leave them.' Yeah.
Man God, look at the suffering on those faces.
Woman Well, if you know you're goin[g t]o die
Man Yeah, it's terrible, isn't it.
Woman Mmm. (yeah) Did they?
Man I don't know. I can't remember in the end. (Neither) Er, it was, it was something about the Hundred Years' War, wasn't it? That was when it took place—about, oh, sometime in the 1300s, I think.
Woman We don't learn those things in America. (laugh)
Man I can't remember my history so . . .
Woman Ask me about the State of California, I can tell you, but . . .
Man Yeah. Let's go over over here towards this one [be]cause I I know this one. This is Rodin's Thinker, isn't it?
Woman I think most people know this one (all right) somehow (right)
Man Gosh, isn't he big.
Woman He's wonderful.
Man Yeah those muscles in his arms. (Mmm) [He']s huge.
Woman What's he thinking about?
Man Mmm, I don't know. I don't know. Perhaps where he left his money. (laugh)
Woman It's one of those ones you can kind of project anything from you on it, you know (Yes) But I suppose he's supposed to be something.
Man Mmm. [I] don't know. An athlete, probably, I mean, he's, look at the size of the legs.

Woman No. He's a, look, he's a serious person. He's just a beautiful serious person. I don't think he's an athlete. (Well) Well athletes don't have brains. (laugh) Sorry. But they don't.

Man Well, I don't know. He's thinking about something anyway. It must be very important to him. Perhaps the catalogue will tell us.

Woman Maybe he's a Greek god or something.

Man Yeah, could be. Yeah.

Woman Zeus?

Man I don't know.

Woman I don't know.

Man Yeah. Perhaps they'll have a catalogue inside, we can go and find out.

Woman Isn't it horrible when you have to buy a catalogue to find out what you're seeing.

Man Yeah.

Woman It's really absurd. (laugh)

Man Let's move on a bit more anyway and see what else there is (OK)

Woman Right.

Man What's that over there?

Woman It's a lump. Oh it's, it's it's Balzac. It's that, yes, (What Balzac?) do you know this one?

Man No.

Woman Well, they commissioned it some, some literary society or something commissioned it (yes) and then they didn't want it after he made it [be]cause they thought it was so awful.

Man So ugly. (mm–hmm) Yeah, it's just a great mass. And that cape doesn't give him any shape at all.

Woman Oh, but it's really strong.

Man Yes, look at the face, the way the head's sort of thrown back.

Woman Those, those really heavy brow arches (yeah) I mean he looks like an individual to be reckoned with (yeah) that's for sure.

Man Yes. So it was a controversial statue, this one, was it?

Woman Mmm. Very. (yeah) Yeah.

Man Maybe it just didn't look like what people thought Balzac looked like.

Woman Well it's not awfully representational is it. I mean it's more of a, an essence than the actual picture. Like The Thinker's really chiselled and . . .

Man It's quite different to The Thinker isn't it. (yeah) I mean The Thinker's got very clean, clear lines and that's sort of just like you said, a sort of lump.

Woman Yeah, it's like clay that just the fingers have just left it almost.

Man Mm. I like that.

Woman So do I.

Man Yeah. I think it's really good. (OK) Look at that one over there in the distance. That sort of arch or what is it? a door or a gate or something.

Woman It looks Renaissance-y, doesn't it.

Man Yes. Oh look, up at the top. There's The Thinker. Right. Can you see?

Woman You're right, yeah.

Man Just up under those three figures on the top. (Well) Now what's The Thinker doing up there?

Woman No, I don't understand this one.

Man And what are those three figures up there? I mean what . . .

Woman Well, OK it looks like the Renaissance, it looks like Hieronymus Bosch a bit, it looks . . .

Man And there's all those angels, are they angels? sort of carved round. It's like one of those . . .

Woman They look like they're falling (mmm) This one's weird.

Man It must tell a story, mustn't it? But goodness knows what the story is and

Woman I've never seen this one before.

Man Perhaps it's . . .

Woman OK. Let's go get the catalogue.

Man Let's go get the catalogue (laugh) we can't stand here all day just looking at this and say[ing] what is it? Yeah. Let's go and get a catalogue and then have a proper look.

Woman Then we can come back maybe.

Man Yeah.

Woman OK.

Section 1 Task 4 (3′ 00″)

Man Right, here's the catalogue that we wanted. Now, let's, let's have a look.

Woman OK. Umm. The first one was The Burghers. Yeah? Let's see. 'Commissioned in 1884' (yeah) mmm, oh here it is. 'To commemorate an event of the Hundred Years' War.'

Man Ah, oh well I had that much right anyway. (You did) Yeah.

Woman 'Calais, blockaded for 11 months in 1346 by Edward III's troops, (Uh huh) sent six of its citizens to sacrifice themselves for the city. Edward was going to execute them but was stopped from doing so by his wife the Queen.'

Man Oh, so they didn't die in the end. (Hmm) I mean, they weren't executed.

Woman No, I guess not. But the statue represents them leaving the city so they thought they were going to be executed.

Man Yeah, oh well that's why they look so sad, isn't it. (mm) What, what does it say about The Thinker?

Woman OK, wait a minute. Mmm. 'The Thinker represents the poet, Dante, meditating upon his creation. Rodin felt that Dante symbolized the artist who is both dreamer and creator.' So I guess that means he's thinking about the *Inferno*.

Man Yeah, well you were right there, weren't you. I mean it . . .

Woman Half right.

Man Well, half right. (laugh) So it isn't a God. (Mm) I, I still don't understand why, you know, a poet like that would be so strong and muscular. I mean, perhaps Dante was a health freak, or something.

Woman (laugh) I don't think so. Umm. Let's see what it says about Balzac. Wait. Yeah, here it is. 'In 1891

Rodin was commissioned by a literary society to do a statue of Balzac.' Mm hmm 'He made many studies for the work which wasn't completed until 1897. When he presented it to the society they were shocked and refused to accept it saying it was 'disrespectful' (Yeah) and looked like a 'melting snowman'.

Man (laugh) Melting snow[man.] It does, doesn't it? It does look like a melting snowman. Yeah.

Woman So, that was the controversy.

Man Yeah, well I suppose the French are fond of Balzac, aren't they, and perhaps they thought that the statue was disrespectful to his memory or something. (Mmm). What about that um that big door thing that we saw?

Woman Yeah, I'm, I'm looking for that. Wait a minute. Ah, here it is. And it is a sort of a door. It's called 'The Gate of Hell.'

Man Oh. Well, yes, I suppo[se] that that's why The Thinker's on it, isn't it? (hm?) I mean, if The Thinker is Dante and the door is Hell then it's, you know, Dante's Inferno.

Woman Listen to this. (The Gates to Hell) 'Rodin's greatest project occupied him for more than 20 years (Oh!) and was left unfinished to his death.'

Man 20 years, can you imagine . . . (Just wait)

Woman 'Nearly 200 figures were made for this Gate of Hell, inspired by Dante's *Inferno*. (Oh) At the top, his head on his hand, is The Thinker, pondering the problem of life and death.'

Man Mmm. I think we did quite well without a catalogue, didn't we. (Yeah) Perhaps we should get a job here as guides or something. (laugh)

Woman Come on. Let's go have a look at the stuff inside.

Man Yeah. OK, then.

Section 2 Task 3 (1' 50")

Man Ooh, look at this, it's a room full of hands.

Woman Oh, they're wonderful.

Man Yeah. Look at this one over here, these two hands coming cupping round each other. 'The Cathedral'. [I]t is like a cathedral, isn't it? Look, you can see right down through the middle of it.

Woman Yeah, the space inside.

Man Yes. It's very sort of open and (Yeah) airy feeling, isn't it.

Woman And, and the shadows are like light coming through stained glass windows (Yes) or something. Yeah.

Man Yeah. Lovely finely done hands, aren't they.

Woman Ooh, I wan[t t]o touch them.

Man (laugh) I don't think they'd like it if you did.

Woman No, I know.

Man No what's this one over here? This huge, it's a huge hand, isn't it, holding this great lump of something.

Woman 'Hand of God.'

Man Mmm. Oh well, yes. Look, round this side, there's um there's two figures. (oh) Must be creating the two (Adam and Eve) Yeah. Adam and Eve being created out of a lump of clay. (yeah) That's nice. I like that. (mm) What a lovely hand.

Woman Very smooth hand, isn't it.

Man Yeah. Yeah.

Woman And over here we have 'The Secret.'

Man The Secret. That's, they're different hands, aren't they, they're very sort of smooth.

Woman Podgy. (Yes) Shorter fingers, not

Man Yeah. Much shorter fingers than the the other one.

Woman But they're a little bit like The Cathedral.

Man Yes, it's the same sort of shape, isn't it.

Woman That's weird. They're right hands. They're not a set.

Man Oh yes, look the thumb is in, yes the thumb . . .

Woman You can't do that with your own hands.

Man No, you can't, can you. (Mm) Look, there's that box inside as well (mm hm) or a cube or a, a I wonder what it is? (a something) Yes, I wonder what that is, what it's supposed to be. That's why they probably call it The Secret. (laugh)

Woman 'cos you're wondering. Yeah. And you'll never find out.

Section 3 Task 2 (1' 43")

Woman Oh, aren't these wonderful. They're so fat and (yes) sweet and you just want to hold them.

Man Look at those little chubby legs.

Woman Cute little kiddies.

Man Oh look, look, this one's got er wings round the back. Yeah, they must be baby angels. (laugh) Aren't they funny. Yes. (mm, Lovely, squishy) Oh, look at this one here. Ah, I think she's lovely. Look at that. She's so, so sweet, just like a . . .

Woman Sweet. Yes she's very s[. . .], no, she's not really my taste. She's a bit . . .

Man Oh, I think she's lovely. She's like those er um girls in Renoir's paintings. She's all sort of . . .

Woman Chocolate box. She, she looks like she'd be good to your face and then do something awful when your back was turned.

Man No, I think she's lovely. Not like this thing over here. Oh, look at this.

Woman That's wonderful.

Man Oh, that's horrible.

Woman It's not!

Man You don't like it, do you?

Woman I love it. It looks Roman, it's strong. I wish the rest of it was there.

Man Yeah, but I it's only half done, I mean there's bits chopped off it all over the place, and the muscles. Look, look . . .

Woman Yes, they're wonderful muscles.

Man But, yes, (They're so . . .) but they're not realistic are they?

Woman Yes, they are.

Man You don't have muscles in places like that.

Woman Well I don't, but you . . . (Well, I don't either) maybe could but don't

Man Nobody has muscles like that.

Woman Yes, they do. It's lovely, strong, it looks Roman. It's wonderful.

Man No. I don't like that.
Woman What do you think of this one?
Man Oooh, it's a bit depressing, isn't it.
Woman Umm. It's very moving though.
Man Yes, yes, it's, no, there's too much suffering in that. I, I don't know. Look at it, (yeah) it's . . .
Woman Briefly in a gallery it's fine.
Man Yes. I wouldn't want to live with it.
Woman You know, I think I've really seen too much today.
Man I have. My feet are tired.
Woman Will you buy me a coffee?
Man Oh, yeah. Let's have a coffee.
Woman OK.
Man Come on then.

CASSETTE 2: SIDE 2
UNIT 7

Section 1 Task 2 (1′ 35″)
. . . in the coming week. And a few exhibitions that I'd like to highlight. The exhibition at the Cleveland Craft Centre shows the work of Philip Webb, an architect from 1831 to 1915. Whilst at the Kirk Leven Old Hall you can see the picture book exhibition until June the twenty-fourth. And in Hartlepool the Gray Art Gallery is showing two photographic exhibitions, the first on experimental photography, and the second called 'Nicaraguan photographs' by Bob Anderson.

It's bonanza time at the Carnaby Raceway this weekend. Don't miss the social highlight of the season, the 'Meet the Riders' disco dance at the Spa Royal Hall, Bridlington. Eight till one. Competitions, including Miss Wet T-shirt. Tickets two pounds, available at the door. Come and meet the country's top road racers.

Come to Auto sixty-six Club's biggest ever motorcycle road race meeting. This Sunday at Carnaby Raceway, Bridlington. See the works Hondas of Australian Wayne Gardner, Roger Marshall and Joey Dunlop, battling with the factory Suzukis of Mick Grant and Rob McElney. Major national solo championship, plus the amazing side-cars. You've seen them on TV, now the superstars come to Carnaby Raceway, Bridlington. Sunday at twelve-thirty.

News now of a fashion show which is taking place tonight at Winterton Rangers Football Club at eight o'clock. Admission is fifty pence and that includes refreshments. They've got a cake stall. They've got a raffle, and all the proceeds will be going to the Fire Service National Benevolent Fund. That is well-worth supporting. A fashion show at Winterton Rangers Football Club tonight. Eight o'clock. Admission 50p, including refreshments. And all proceeds are going to the er . . . Fire Service National Benevolent Fund.

Section 1 Task 4 (0′ 25″)
The City of York got a royal visit today when Prince Charles arrived to open the latest tourist attraction, a tenth century Viking village. Jorvik is a two and a half million pound reconstruction of a Viking settlement, which has taken more than two years to develop. Since its opening to the public a month ago, sixty thousand people have visited the site, and the organizers are extremely excited about the response.

Section 2 Task 2 (0′ 27″)
The site itself produced a . . . a very different picture of the Viking than the . . . the general one we have. Here we saw the Viking man in the street and not the Viking man in the ship. Not the Viking pirate, the raider, but the Viking trader. So this was a totally new idea of the Vikings as entrepreneurs, as commercial geniuses, as many of them were.

Section 2 Tasks 3 and 4 (0′ 40″)
There was local trade and then there was international trade, erm . . . they were bringing in wine from the Rhineland, or jewellery from the Rhineland. They were bringing in amber from the Baltic to make into amber jewellery, so quite . . . a wide range of contacts. Some of those are just luxury products for consumption here. Some of them are raw materials to be turned into things in . . . in Coppergate by the craftsmen. But they were enjoying a very comfortable standard of living — nice houses, nice things to use, good food. They would be very comfortably off by our standards.

Section 2 Task 6 (0′ 20″)
There was so much excitement about the village buried at the heart of York that it was decided to reconstruct a whole street, and people it with life-size models of Vikings at work. Visitors go round the street in small, electronically-controlled cars, which the staff say travel through time into the tenth century.

Section 2 Task 7 (4′ 43″)
OK, we've arrived in Jorvik now, 948 A.D. . . . Well, this is the erm person who makes wooden bowls and things like that. Oh, look at those enormous eggs — fish, (Man: Oysters) oysters? Oh, yeah! What are they doing? Oh, it's the erm . . . the shoemaker — makes leather shoes. And what's this man? (Man: Jewellery) Oh, he makes jewellery, yes. He's got some nice things. Oh, what's he doing? He's making something. They're all . . . er . . . these are all workshops, where people make things. Oh . . . we're go . . . Oh, we're going into a house now. (Man: Yes) This is the hearth. A hearth is a . . . means er . . . the fireplace. Everything happens in the same room. She's making bread, I think. There's a man talking. Oh, this is a loom. A loom is erm . . . a thing for making, for weaving wool for making cloth. (Man: Very interesting) Is that a pig in there? (Man: Yes) Oh, look at this (laughs) this is the cesspit. It's the (Man: It's the loo.) . . . Viking loo, yeah, Viking toilet. The man in the toilet doesn't look very well. I think he's been drinking too much. Phew, it doesn't smell very nice. Here's the boat coming in. There's a wool shop. (Man: look, the anchor) Oh, yeah. Oh, that's a strange anchor, yeah. Ah there's two fishermen telling stories to a young boy. T . . . telling him about their adventures on the sea and everything. This is a fisherman's hut. Ah, now we're coming back to 1980. This is the archaeological excavation work.

Section 2 Task 8 (2′ 02″)

On the right skins are pinned to the wall, and on the left there's a . . . a bench where obviously a Viking would be working on the leather. From time to time Magnus Magnusson's resonant voice speaks through a loud speaker behind your ear with a commentary. Presumably this was a couple of kids trying to sell me something, I'm not quite sure what. There's so much going on that er . . . even with Mis . . . Mister Magnusson talking in the background it's a bit tricky to . . . to know what the people are doing. On the right at the moment there's a . . . a loom where people — Vikings would have er . . . woven wool. And behind me there's a . . . a domestic hearth scene with people cooking bread on a . . . an open fire. Coming up on the left is the cesspit, and apparently this has er . . . got a real special effect in er . . . that you can smell it as you go past. Yes . . . I can smell something. (laughs) No, it doesn't smell very nice at all in fact. And the man sitting in the cesspit has got a very red nose. It looks as if he's having a hard time. A little further we came across a fishing boat with men singing as they worked. . . . At the end of the time tunnel is a display of Viking buildings — wattle and wood, twisted and woven to form the frames of walls. And then the time travel is over.

UNIT 8

Section 1 Task 1 (3′ 13″)

Wally Today is Tuesday, May 29, 5.32 a.m. Morning, Larry.

Larry Good morning, Wally. First of all, we always look for lost children early in the morning. Maybe we can help Mary Adams. Mary Adams is from Maryland. For those people that are in the vicinity of 2900 South on the Dan Ryan, Mary Adams was driving on the Dan Ryan, 2900 South, when her dog jumped from the car. Now it's a Belgian sheepdog. It's black in color. It's 24 inches from ground to shoulder, and if you're fortunate enough to get close enough to it, it has a tattoo in its right ear. The tattoo is J for John, R for Robert, R for Robert, and then there's a number. The dog answers to the name of Desiree. It's not your local pooch, Wally. The dog is valued at $25,000.
So if you're looking for me later today, I will be in the vicinity of 2900 South on the Dan Ryan looking for Desiree, because uh . . .

Wally Well I won't be here, I'll be out there wi . . . with you.

Larry Well, I['ve] got a faster car than you do, and you can't leave till ten o'clock, so I['ve] got a little head start on you. We're gonna be lookin[g] for Desiree all morning Wally. We'll get back to you from the scene.

Wally All right, Larry. Thanks.

Wally We're at twenty-two minutes to six exactly in Chicago, officially. Desiree, a Belgian sheepdog. Black, he said. It stands 24 inches ground to shoulder, tattoo in the ear. I don't think I'd want to check that out without . . .

Second man What does that mean?

Wally Well it means Desiree might not want you to get too close to check out the tattoo in her ear, obviously. Not obviously but I guess it's a she, Desiree is the name. Well we've had all kinds of happenings in the big city of Chicago. Never a missing $25,000 dog before, never to our knowledge. 29th and the Dan Ryan, that vicinity. Are you interested, or are you in the area? Maybe you're on the Dan Ryan, or in your car, you could keep a[n] eye peeled for that, be worthwhile and, uh . . . if you want to get in touch with us, that should be easy. We'll take care of the arrangements to get it back to her, the visitor from Maryland who lost her dog, $25,000 worth of dog.

It's 5.47 in Chicago. We're still looking for a $25,000 dog. Sounds funny, but I mean a . . . a Belgian sheepdog, worth that amount. It got out of its car, or its owner's car, on the Dan Ryan at 29th sometime this morning, and is on the loose. Desiree is the name. It's [a] black Belgian sheepdog. If you're finding it, I imagine there would be a nice reward attached, I guess.

It's ten to six now, five-five-oh a.m. Well, [it]'d be nice if we can help the lady from Maryland recover her Belgian sheepdog, last seen: Dan Ryan near 29th street.

Six o'clock in the morning. No, we're still on the look out, be on the look out for a Belgian sheepdog, black, uh . . . 24 inches ground to shoulder is the description, name: Desiree; worth two thou . . . $25,000.

Section 1 Task 2 (2′ 12″)

Wally Five after six. We do have an APB, as Jack Webb would say, out this morning for a Belgian sheepdog who is worth $25,000, who got out of a car on the Dan Ryan near 29th street and uh . . . is on the loose apparently. Good morning, Barbara.

Barbara Hi.

Wally How are you?

Barbara I'm just fine.

Wally You know this dog, eh?

Barbara Well, I know her by reputation. I was sitting in my kitchen looking at some Belgian sheepdog newsletters.

Wally Um hm.

Barbara One of them has a picture of Desiree on the cover. And, uh . . . so I thought maybe you'd like some background on why she's worth so much.

Wally Why is she worth $25,000?

Barbara Well, the reason she was travelling through the area, we held our national specialty in Minneapolis on Sunday.

Wally Um hm.

Barbara So, she was travelling home. Now, she did not win this year's specialty, but she won the 1983 specialty . . .

Wally Mmm.

Barbara . . . in Las Vegas. So, she's a beautiful dog. She's ah . . . she was imported from Belgium. So . . .

Wally Describe her again so people who might be driving around today would have a good uh . . . description.

Barbara Right. She's solid black. She has prick ears, that means they stand up. She has a very long, black coat, very long, luxurious black tail.

Wally Um hm.

Barbara Hopefully she's wearing a collar.

Wally How much does she weigh, approximately?

Barbara All right, I would say she probably weighs in the area of 55–60 pounds.

Wally Is she friendly? Are the Belgian sheepdogs . . .

Barbara Oh, Sh . . . Belgian sheepdogs are very friendly, but of course being out loose like this she may be a little spooked by the cars, or . . .

Wally Um hm.

Barbara . . . something like that, but (Well we certainly . . .) certainly she's basically friendly.

Wally We want to find her for her health's sake, and uh . . .

Barbara Her call name is Desi.

Wally Desi?

Barbara Right.

Wally Um hm. Well . . .

Barbara So that would help too. I think if she heard her name she might come.

Wally Well, we've got everybody marshalled to help here, so we'll keep an eye out, both of [th]em, for Desi.

Barbara Desi.

Wally Desiree from . . .

Barbara Right.

Wally . . . from Maryland.

Barbara From Maryland.

Wally And her owner, Mary Adams.

Barbara Mary Linda Adams.

Wally Mary Linda Adams. Hope we can help her because she'd like to go back home remembering Chicago as the place where hospitable people helped find her dog.

Barbara Oh, I hope so too.

Wally Well we'll work on it.

Barbara OK. Bye.

Wally Thank you. Bye

Section 1 Task 3 (0′ 57″)

Wally It's 6.15 exactly in Chicago. Pat, good morning.

Pat Hi.

Wally Yes.

Pat How are you?

Wally Good. How are you?

Pat Oh fine. I just heard you on uh the radio, the lady [th]at called?

Wally About the sheepdog?

Pat Yeah.

Wally Yeah.

Pat Well you know what, my daughter was on the Dan Ryan, and she saw this dog, and she slowed down. And all at when she slowed down, a car hit her and four other cars.

Wally No kidding.

Pat Yes. N . . . now whether it was a sheepdog . . .

Wally When was this?

Pat This was uh yesterday afternoon.

Wally Oh no, this . . .

Pat About . . . huh?

Wally No this is this morning the dog got away.

Pat Oh this was this morning.

Wally That had to be another guy.

Pat Oh.

Wally I'm sorry. Is your daughter all right?

Pat Uh . . . well, we haven't talked to her, the last time we talked she was lying down.

Wally Mmm . . .

Pat But you know she came . . . picked the dog up at the Dan Ryan, and took it to the animal shelter. (Did she?) The police wouldn't even take the dog.

Wally Isn't that nice of her?

Pat Yeah.

Wally What's her name?

Pat Uh, Carolyn Schlaffer.

Wally Well I hope she's OK.

Pat Oh, I hope so too.

Wally Thank you.

Pat Thank you.

Wally Mm hm.

Section 1 Tasks 5 and 6 (1′ 03″)

Wally It's 6.23. Well, I don't know if this was the dog or not but Bill you said you saw a black dog yesterday. What time?

Bill Yes sir. We were, uh going uh east, on uh Kennedy expressway about two o'clock, and the dog was uh . . . on the right hand side so he was headin[g] out towards O'Hare airfield.

Wally Where on the Kennedy?

Bill Uh . . . between Canfield, and uh . . . maybe Harlem.

Wally Which is a far spell from where he got out of the car, if it was twenty-ninth and Dan Ryan.

Bill Yeah he was about uh, like you say, about 24 inches high . . .

Wally Um hm.

Bill . . . black, and he was loping along, and he looked like a sheepdog . . .

Wally Mmm.

Bill . . . long black hair.

Wally Long black hair.

Bill Um hm.

Wally Well that's a possibility. And what time was this?

Bill About two o'clock (two) yesterday afternoon.

Wally We'll sure make a note of it.

Bill OK.

Wally And that involves people who are all the way from 29th and Ryan out to O'Hare then. Thanks.

Bill He was lopin[g] along at a pretty good speed.

Wally Thanks very much.

Bill OK.

Wally Some place in this huge city is a very valuable dog on the loose. $25,000 worth of Belgian sheepdog, a prize-winner, as you heard.

Section 2 Task 1 (1′ 01″)

Wally It's 6.28 in Chicago, they're to give you a report on what's been going on here, from Larry Schriner. Larry?

Larry Good morning, Wally. Mary Adams, 36 years old from Maryland, on the Dan Ryan expressway on 2900 South late yesterday afternoon we are now told. We apologize for the change in that time. We were given incorrect information. Her Belgian sheepdog jumped from her car. The do... the dog, black in color, 24 inches from the ground to the shoulder, has a tattoo in his or her right ear. The initials are J for John, R for Robert, R for Robert and then there's a number. We don't have the number at the present time. The dog['s] valued at $25,000.

Wally Let me stop you one second Larry. What time did this happen, now do you know, yesterday afternoon?

Larry The police uh ... called back Wally, they didn't have the exact time when we first called. They tell us it was around three o'clock yesterday afternoon.

Section 2 Task 2 (0′ 30″)

Twenty-six minutes to seven right now, in Chicago. That's the case that we're working on right now, a dog on ... Incidentally we talked to a woman before whose daughter had seen one yesterday and stopped her car and was involved in an accident because of it. We'd like to hear from you again, Pat, if you'll call us, because Larry Schriner would like to check out all the details of that one too, and uh ... you may have more to offer than we originally thought. All right Pat, get back to us, and you and your daughter Carolyn, we'd like to talk to you.

Section 2 Task 3 (3′ 00″)

Wally It's 6.44 a.m. and Carolyn had a scene yesterday. Now, Carolyn ... where were you on the Dan Ryan when this happened?

Carolyn Uh, yes I was. I was I was comin[g] back from um ... dropping off a car, on ... uh ... over at Keystone Chevrolet (Um hm) and we were driving back, me and my fiance ...

Wally Um hm.

Carolyn And I see about 500 feet up ahead that there was this black dog walking right across the lanes of the Dan Ryan.

Wally Oh, oh, that may be our dog.

Carolyn Yeah, and uh ... and what had happened was, I stopped and the cars behind me, you know how it goes, on the slippery pavement ...

Wally Yeah.

Carolyn ... uh they all just went sliding into everybody, (Um hm) and it turned out to be a four car crash up.

Wally W... were you hurt though?

Carolyn Well no. I just ... no I'm fine, you know.

Wally It's a traumatic thing, naturally.

Carolyn Yeah, specially if you've never been in an accident before.

Wally Mm hm.

Carolyn But uh ... you know, and then we ... you know we got the dog ... and we and I got the dog ... I got him by the collar right? ... and a tow-truck guy was gonna take him and just put him on the side you know, on the side of the road, to let him go ... ?

Wally Yeah?

Carolyn ... and he comes runnin[g] back onto the expressway again, almost caused another accident ...

Wally So whatever happened to him?

Carolyn Well I took him in the car, you know, and then ... the whole police thing and everything, and we got the report filled out and all that, and then they let me go, and we took the ... uh ... took the dog to a ... animal shelter on 61st and Wabasn.

Wally 61st and Wabash.

Carolyn Um hm.

Wally OK.

Carolyn Now this dog, I don't know if ... you know, I don't know what kind of dog he is.

Wally Well let me ask you if he, he was he about ... uh 24 inches high, would you say 2 feet, and ...

Carolyn Oh yeah.

Wally ... weighed about 50–55 pounds? (Sure.) Long black hair?

Carolyn Sure. Long black hair, he had a collar on. All black.

Wally Ears that stand up?

Carolyn He had a wh... a black collar on. I'm sorry?

Wally The ears stand up?

Carolyn Did his ears stand up? Yeah they did.

Wally Ah, I think that's our guy.

Carolyn Yeah.

Wally I'm sorry for what happened to you, but obviously you only uh ... had it happen because you were concerned about the dog, otherwise you wouldn't have stopped.

Carolyn That's right.

Wally And that's an indication of how you care.

Carolyn Oh, sure.

Wally So I hope that this is factual, but I think that's the dog that belongs to a woman from uh ... Maryland who was displaying the dog and showing him up in Minneapolis, was on her way back, and the dog is an outstanding dog because it's a national prize winner.

Carolyn Oh, really?

Wally Yeah. It's a she. Her name is Desiree.

Carolyn It was a she because when we took him in, you know, the ... the guy was checking. He said this is a she.

Wally Desi is her name. Desiree.

Carolyn Desiree.

Wally So she's still at the animal shelter, sixty ...

Carolyn Yes, she is.

Wally 61st and Wabash.

Carolyn That's right. Er ...

Wally We'd better get out there right away, (Yeah) and see if we can get hold of somebody there.

Carolyn Yeah, um.

Wally Well, Carolyn, nice of you to do it. I'm glad you're OK. Sorry about your accident but, (Oh.) hold on we want to ... what's your last name again?

Carolyn Uh ... Schlaffer.

Wally I talked to your mom before.

Carolyn Right, right. (laughs) If she calls me this early again . . .

Wally She has a great taste in daughters, believe me . . .

Carolyn Oh, I'm . . . I'm glad that um . . . you know . . .

Wally . . . and vice versa.

Carolyn . . . found the owner, you know . . .

Wally We'll take your number here, I wan[t t]o get back to you. Hold on a second.

Carolyn OK.

Section 2 Task 4 (0′ 21″)

We'd like to visit the uh . . . Animal Welfare League this morning if we can to see about our friend Desiree, so maybe, we can solve our mystery and uh . . . return Desi to her owner here. If we can get in touch with the animal shelter . . . we'll have to get call information to get the name, uh . . . the phone number for that place at 61st and Wabash.

Section 2 Task 5 (0′ 50″)

Wally It's twelve minutes to seven. Good morning Bob.

Bob I just *come* in here, sir. I really haven't had a chance to look and see what's here or nothin[g]. [Th]at's *like* I told the lady when I just, I just walked in the door.

Wally All right, we'll . . .

Bob I don't even . . . supposed to start to work until seven o'clock.

Wally I apologize for bustin[g] in on you. We were tryin[g] to get the good news for the owner of the dog.

Bob Yeah. Well if . . . if I['ve] got one in here, you can call me back in about 25 or 30 minutes and I can definitely tell you whether the dog is here or not.

Wally We will be glad to call you back. We . . . did . . . did the lady tell you what we're looking for?

Bob Yes, (OK) a Belgian shepherd.

Wally Belgian sheepdog, Bob.

Bill I have had about four different calls right behind it al . . .

Wally Oh, really? I'm sorry. Well, uh . . . we'll give you our number if you want to call us back, or we'll call you back.

Bob Well you can call me back, would be . . . probably be better.

Section 2 Task 6 (1′ 00″)

Wally We'll in a few minutes, I guess, ascertain whether or not this is the dog, but I think it is. Just again quickly, yesterday a woman from Maryland is driving back from Minneapolis through Chicago in the midst of the bad weather we're having, and on at . . . Dan Ryan and 29th Street her dog jumps out of the car. It's a very valuable prize-winning Belgian sheepdog, worth $25,000. If you can evaluate an animal that wins awards like that, and of course you can picture her distress . . . well, that was on our police report this morning, to try to find the dog, both for her sake and to keep the dog safe as well, and this is probably the right answer, that it was taken by Carolyn, our caring friend, to the Animal Welfare League, but as you heard he just got to

work. He's got to look around all the ones that are . . . presently being cared for there, and see if this is so.

Woman Oh, I certainly hope so.

Wally Well you can rest assured nothing will happen to her now, because obviously that's what that place is all about, animal and welfare. It's four minutes to seven exactly in Chicago. It is uh . . . Tuesday May 29.

UNIT 5

Section 1 Task 3

Quotation a (Extract 2)
Winston Churchill, British Prime Minister, describing the 'Soviet sphere'. 5 March 1946

Quotation b (Extract 1)
Neil Armstrong, American astronaut, describing the first walk on the moon. 20 July 1969.

Quotation c
Muhammad Ali (born Cassius Clay) when he was World Heavyweight Boxing Champion in 1966.

Quotation d (Extract 4)
Martin Luther King, civil rights leader, at the Poor People's march on Washington. 28 August 1963.

Quotation e
Attributed to John Lennon, talking about the Beatles in the early 1960s.

Quotation f (Extract 3)
John F. Kennedy, American President, in his inaugural address. 20 January 1961.

Quotation g (Extract 5)
Edward VIII, British King, in his abdication speech from Windsor Castle. 11 December 1936.